Local citizen; global citizen

Contents

Authors: Margot Brown, Centre for Global Education, York and Diana Durie, Development Education Centre (South Yorkshire)

Design & Illustration: King Graphics
Cover photo: Christian Aid/Elaine Duigenan
© Christian Aid 2000

ISBN: 0 904379 46 9

About Christian Aid

An agency of the churches in the UK and Ireland, Christian Aid works wherever the need is greatest, regardless of religion. It works in over 60 countries worldwide through local organisations that understand local needs.

Christian Aid believes in strengthening people to find their own solutions to the problems they face. It strives for a world transformed by an end to poverty and campaigns to change the rules that keep people poor.

Acknowledgements

This pack has been revised and adapted from *The People G.R.I.D.,* first published in 1977 by Oxfam and Cockpit Arts Workshop (ILEA). The original material was based on the work of Alec Davison, then Director of the Cockpit Arts Workshop, and Margot Brown, then Education Adviser for Oxfam, North London. Our thanks to Alec Davison and Oxfam for permission to revise and extend the original material.

We are also grateful to Sue Tite, Head of Teacher Education, College of Ripon & York, and Katie Duckworth, previously Children's Education Adviser at Christian Aid, for their help in developing the pack.

Thanks also to Stephanie Twilley (Teacher), Gill Sparks (Education Officer, Kent Wildlife Trust), and Isobel Perry (Co-ordinator, Kent and the Wider World resource centre) for their useful comments and suggestions.

Many children and teachers have contributed to the final version through testing in the classroom. Our special thanks to:

Bryn Jones and children, Copmanthorpe Junior School, York; Lynn Markham and children, Dunnington C of E Primary School, York; Joanna Keeley, Alexia Dawson, Li Rose and children, Hambleton School, North Yorkshire; Tracy Levitt and Richard Turner and children, Holme-on-Spalding Moor Primary School, North Yorkshire; Steve Halksworth and children, Huntington Primary School, York; Sue Gore and children, Mansel Primary School, Sheffield; Fiona Brunt and children, Marlcliffe Primary School, Sheffield; Val Wyman and children, Poppleton Road School, York; Malcolm Appleby and Douglas Kidd and children, Warter Primary School, North Yorkshire; and Ayal Demissis, Sheffield.

Finally, a special thanks to Susan Bainbridge for tirelessly typing many drafts of the text.

CENTRE FOR GLOBAL EDUCATION

Development Education Centre (South Yorkshire)

Introduction

Aknowledge and understanding of the concepts central to life are an important part of learning. If children are to be prepared for opportunities, responsibilities and experiences as active citizens, they will need a range of skills and values. These will help children understand the knowledge they gain of the world around them.

This pack aims to help children explore and comprehend the concepts of growth and development, interdependence and relationships – in contexts ranging from the individual to the global. To help them understand the changing world in which they are growing up, it is important that they recognise the way everyday life in their own communities affects, and is affected by, the wider world.

Introduction

How to use the pack

The pack is divided into three self-contained but interlinked units. While each unit can be used on its own, they are all structured to show the progression from the individual, personal level to the global level (fig 1).

Each unit consists of a core simulation activity (see page 5). In addition, there are several introductory activities that help set the scene and introduce one or more of the key ideas related to the core activity. There are also follow-up activities to use with the core activity, including case studies based on experiences of children around the world. All the introductory and follow-up activities are self-contained and can be used on their own or with other themes or topics.

Citizenship, personal and social development

All the activities involve children talking to each other, working together and making decisions both as a group and as individuals. Through this interaction, children develop skills of citizenship and grow as individuals and as a group. This education of the whole child is stressed in England in the framework for Personal, Social and Health Education and Citizenship at Key Stages 1 and 2 (1999, DFEE and QCA); in the Scottish Personal and Social Development Guidelines (1993) with the related document, The *Heart of the Matter* (1994); and in the Personal and Social Education framework, Key Stages 1 and 2, in Wales (2000, ACCAC). The pack works as a programme of PSHE (England), PSD (Scotland) and PSE (Wales) as outlined in the table on page 7. There are occasional cross-references between the units to help identify progression, learning links and common themes.

Notes

1. We have tried to be as historically and geographically accurate as possible when referring to the five jurisdictions contained in the British Isles. The 'UK' refers to England, Scotland, Wales and Northern Ireland. When also referring to the Republic of Ireland, the term 'UK and Ireland' is used.

2. When we refer to UK law, we recognise that the four countries of the UK do not share the same legal system.

| INDIVIDUAL | COMMUNITY | WORLD |
| Growing up | Word house | Global cake |

Figure 1

Progression through
Local Citizen; Global Citizen

Local citizen; global citizen
Introduction

Learning through simulation

Simulation is a way of learning that allows children to make decisions, experience feelings and see the results of those decisions in a structured environment. Simulation activities do not involve children taking on a role or attempting to become someone else. Children participate and make decisions as themselves.

Simulations are not exact models of real-life situations. Instead, they provide a setting in which children, by interacting with each other, experience what a real-life situation might be like. Every child's contribution is vital and relevant. It is important to plan enough time after completing the simulation to reflect on what has happened. An experience of success, frustration, enjoyment or problem-solving promotes a greater understanding of related issues outside the classroom.

The core simulation activities in each unit involve the whole class and are structured so that every child participates as an individual, as well as a member of a pair or a group. Learning happens through interaction between children, doing a task, making joint decisions, reflecting and making connections. The combination of individual and group activities, practical and mental involvement makes simulation a very enjoyable way to learn.

How simulation works in Local Citizen; Global Citizen	1: Growing up	2: Word house	3: Global cake
The whole class...	...represents an environment for five years of a person's life.	...becomes a street of families that have moved to Britain over the centuries and have added words from their languages to English.	...represents a world community that is involved in providing ingredients for a huge global cake. The end product is a class mural of the ingredients and baking process.
Groups...	...of children are responsible for the growth of all aspects of one imaginary person, including physical, social and emotional.	...of children become one of eight families who have added words to the English language. Pairs of children have to show that they understand other families' words.	...of differing sizes represent regions of the world that provide ingredients for the cake.
Simulation of...	...life experiences that affect growth.	...the encounters people have with each other, primarily through buying and selling and the impact such encounters have on sharing language.	...the links that regions of the world and people have with each other through global trade.
Reflection on...	...life experiences and successful or frustrating bartering.	...the development of language and literacy, visiting different people and undertaking interesting research.	...experiences of frustration or success, unfairness and good teamwork.
Links with issues such as...	...healthy exercise and good diet aiding physical growth, while bereavement, illness or accident may impede development.	...the development of language and literacy, and the history of Britain and movements of people.	...fair trade and pay.

Introduction

Route through the introductory, core and follow-up activities

Start here

1: Growing up — *Focus on the individual*

Introductory activities
- Each person has a unique identity.
- Names are an important part of people's identity.
- There are different naming traditions around the world.

Follow-up activities
- Similarities and differences between children growing up around the world.
- Work and play, roles and responsibilities.

Core activity key themes

Growth:	physical, emotional, social, moral, intellectual.
Relationships:	with people, institutions, resources.
Interdependence:	links with individuals, family, school and community.
Development:	personal growth and change.

2: Word house — *Focus on communities*

Introductory activities
- Communication.
- Languages change.
- Stories about one original language from which many languages developed.

Follow-up activities
- Children and their families leave home and move elsewhere in the world for a range of reasons.
- People who move to the UK bring their spoken and written languages with them.

Core activity key themes

Growth:	the English language grew as a result of invasion, settlement, trade and immigration.
Relationships:	between languages and the movement of people.
Interdependence:	links and connections between peoples through language.
Development:	languages grow and change through encounters.

3: Global cake — *Focus on the world*

Introductory activities
- Fairness and unfairness explored.

Follow-up activities
- Children at work in the UK and around the world.
- Consumers in the UK are linked to the rest of the world through what they buy.

Core activity key themes

Growth:	economic wealth can be created through trade; the gap between rich and poor.
Relationships:	not all relationships are fair and just.
Interdependence:	trade and work link people together.
Development:	how trade affects growth and change in countries.

Introduction

Curriculum links

The units in *Local Citizen; Global Citizen* are for use with children between 8 and 12 years old for a range of abilities and language levels.

England	*Northern Ireland*	*Scotland*	*Wales*
English Speaking and listening Reading Writing	**English** Talking and listening Reading Writing	**English** Listening Talking Reading Writing	**English** Talking and listening Reading
Mathematics Number Shape, space and measures Data handling	**Mathematics** Processes Number Handling data	**Mathematics** Information handling	**Mathematics** Number Shape, space and measures
Science Life processes and living things Materials and their properties	**Science** Living things	**Science** Understanding living things and the processes of life	**Science** Living things and life processes
History Historical interpretation Historical enquiry Local, British and world history	**History** Developing knowledge, understanding and skills	**Environmental studies** Understanding people in the past	**History** Historical interpretation Historical enquiry Local, British and world history
Geography Recognise how places fit with a wider context Themes: environment, settlement	**Geography** Developing knowledge, understanding and skills Where people live What people do Environment	**Environmental studies** Understanding people and place Understanding people in society Health education Technology: developing informed attitudes	**Geography** Understanding people and place Recognise how places fit with a wider context
RE Learn from religions: co-operation, equality, fairness, justice, rules and human rights, individual and community	**RE** Morality Respect for others Caring and sharing	**Religious and moral education** Relationships and moral values	**RE** Learn from religions: co-operation, equality, fairness, justice, rules and human rights, individual and community
Personal, social and health education, and citizenship Confidence and responsibility Active role as citizens Healthy lifestyle Respect differences between people	**Health education**	**Personal and social development** Self-awareness Self-esteem Inter-personal relationships Independence and interdependence	**Personal and social education** Social aspect, community aspect physical aspect, emotional aspect moral aspect, vocational aspect learning aspect
Cross-curricular themes Enterprise education Financial capability	**Cross-curricular themes** Education for mutual understanding Cultural heritage	**Cross-curricular themes** Multicultural and anti-racist education Enterprise education	**Cross-curricular themes** Economic and industrial understanding Community understanding

Introduction

Suggestions for using the case studies

Asking questions

Give each pair of children a copy of just one of the case studies to read and to devise a series of questions about it. The case studies can be exchanged with other pairs and the questions answered.

Press conference

Divide the class into four groups and use one case study to set up a newspaper interview. All the children read the case study and one person from each group takes the role of the child in the story. The rest of the group are journalists. They ask questions and write down the answers, and at the end of the 'press conference' the journalists write up the interview for their newspaper. The interviewees can write about being interviewed.

The groups can use Information and Communication Technology to produce a newspaper article.

Things in common

Divide the class into small groups and give each group one of the case studies. Together the children can make a list of things they have in common with the person in the story. What do they think that person will do in the future? What do they think they themselves will do in the future?

Writing a letter

Compose a letter to an aid organisation to find out more about the work they do for children. Choose an organisation whose work is appropriate to the unit being used. See page 10 for a list of useful addresses.

NB: Only send one letter from the class to avoid workers in these organisations being swamped by letters needing a reply.

Children's Charter

Ask the class to discuss problems that children may have. How can they be cared for and protected? What would make life better for all of them? Turn the suggestions into a Charter for Children.

Would it be the same for each of the children in the case studies? Does anything need to be changed or added? Children can compare their charter with the Convention on the Rights of the Child (below).

Case studies

UN Convention on the Rights of the Child, Article 32

The child has the right to be protected from economic exploitation and from performing any work that is likely to be hazardous or interfere with the child's education.

Introduction

Further resources

1: Growing up

For the classroom

Daniel and the Mischief Boy – true stories of an African family
(1993) Christian Aid/Harper Collins, London

Feeling Good about Faraway Friends
(1995) Leeds Development Education Centre, Leeds

Living and Learning in a Tanzanian Village – a child's perspective
(1992, Update 1996) Manchester Development Education Project, Manchester

Isatou, Chloe and You
(1994) Wiltshire World Studies Centre, Marlborough

Lima Lives – children in a Latin American city
(1993) Save The Children, London

Changing Childhoods: British social history since 1930
(1996) Save The Children, London

Our World, Our Rights
(1996) Amnesty International UK, London

Values and Visions – a handbook for spiritual development and global awareness
(1995) Hodder & Stoughton/Christian Aid/Manchester DEP Ltd, London

The Great Games Book
(1997) Adams, S, Dorling Kindersley London

Talking Drum – classroom ideas for teaching 4- to 9-year-olds based on stories from India, Nigeria, China and Peru
(1996) Christian Aid/SCIAF, London

My Name is Harriet
(1990) Osrin & Walasek, Walker Books & J S Sainsbury, London

The Rights of the Child set (The Whole Child; It's Our Right; Keep Us Safe)
Save the Children and UNICEF UK, London

The Number on My Grandfather's Arm
(1987) Adler, D, UAHC Press (NY) Available from Jewish Education Bureau, 8 Westcombe Avenue, Leeds LS8 2BS

For the teacher

Children as Citizens: Education for Participation
(1998) Holden, C and Clough, N (eds), Jessica Kingsley Publishers, London

The Wordsworth Dictionary of First Names
(1995) McCleod, I and Freedman, T, Wordsworth Reference, Ware

Scottish Christian Names (sic)
(1978, 1988, reprinted 2000) Dunkling, L Johnston and Bacon, Stirling

State of the World's Children
(2000, published annually) UNICEF, London

The Right to Play and Children's participation in Article 3 Action Pack – Children's Rights and Children's Play
(1994) Hart, R, Playtrain, Birmingham

Children's Participation. The Theory and Practice of Involving Young Citizens in Community Development and Environmental Care
(1997) Hart, R, UNICEF and Earthscan

2: Word house

For the classroom

Eritrea: Africa's newest country – a locality study for Primary Schools
(1993) Christian Aid, London

Let's Cooperate
Mildred Masheder, Peace Education Project, London

Learning Together; global education 4-7
(1990) Fountain and WWF, Cheltenham

The Surprise Party
(1981) Pat Hutchins, Puffin, London

Don't Forget the Bacon
(1981) Pat Hutchins, Puffin, London

Refugees – a resource book for 8- to 13-year-olds
(1998) Rutter, J, Refugee Council London

For the teacher

The Future of English
(1998) Graddol, D, The British Council, London

The Languages of the World
(1977) Katzner, K, Routledge and Kegan Paul, London

Third World Atlas Second Edition
(1994) Thomas, A et al, Open University Press

The English Language
(1985) Robert Burchfield, Open University Press

What's in a Word – vocabulary development in multilingual classrooms
(1998) Norah McWilliam, Trentham Books, Stoke-on-Trent

Mother Tongue: the English language
(1990, re-issued 2000) Bill Bryson, Penguin, London

Roots of the Future: ethnic diversity in the making of Britain
(1996) Commission for Racial Equality, London

Voices series
(1995) edited by Warner, R, Minority Rights Group, London

Forging New Identities – young refugees and minority students tell their stories
(1998) Minority Rights Group, London

3: Global cake

For the classroom

Feeling Good About Faraway Friends
(1995) Leeds Development Education Centre, Leeds

For People and Planet; an active learning pack for KS2
(1992) Bellett, E and Philbrick, M, Traidcraft Exchange, Newcastle

It's Not Fair – a handbook on world development for youth groups
(1993) Christian Aid, London

New Journeys (Kenya and Tanzania).
(1991) Development Education Centre, Birmingham

The Paper Bag Game
(revised 1996) Christian Aid, London

The World in a Supermarket Bag
(1987) Oxfam, Oxford

Children of the Loom – school worship leaflet
(1994) Christian Aid, London

People Friendly Coffee – leaflet
(1993) Christian Aid, London

Global Gang – a free quarterly newspaper packed full of lively features, puzzles and competitions
Christian Aid, London

For the teacher

Education for Development – a teachers' resource for global learning
(1995) Susan Fountain, UNICEF/Hodder & Stoughton, London

The Politics of The Real World
(1994) Jacobs, M, Earthscan, London

How the World Works – an Oxfam guide
(1992) Thorpe, D and Potts, A, Oxford

A Sporting Chance: tackling child labour in India's sports goods industry
(1997) Christian Aid, London

The Globe-Trotting Sports Shoe
(1995) Brookes, B and Madden, P, Christian Aid, London

The Hidden Army – children at work in the 1990s
(1991) Pond, C and Searle, A, Low Pay Unit and Birmingham City Council, Education Department, London

Third World Atlas Second Edition
(1994) Thomas, A et al, Open University Press

Introduction

Useful addresses

ActionAid
Hamlyn House
Macdonald Road
Archway
London N19 5PG

Tel: 020 7561 7561
Website: www.actionaid.org

Amnesty International
United Kingdom
99-119 Rosebery Avenue
London EC1R 4RE

Tel: 020 7814 6200
Website: www.amnesty.org.uk

Anti-Slavery International
Thomas Clarkson House
The Stableyard
Broomgrove Road
London SW9 9TL

Tel: 020 7501 8920
Website: www.antislavery.org

CAFOD
2 Romero Close
Stockwell Road
London SW9 9TY

Tel: 020 7733 7900
Website: www.cafod.org.uk

Centre for Global Education
College of Ripon & York
Lord Mayor's Walk
York YO31 7EX

Tel: 01904 716839

Christian Aid
Website: www.christian-aid.org.uk

PO Box 100
London SE1 7RT
Tel: 020 7620 4444

30 Wellington Park
Belfast BT9 6DL
Tel: 028 9038 1204

PO Box 21
Cardiff CF14 2DL
Tel: 029 2061 4435

PO Box 11
Edinburgh EH1 1EL
Tel: 0131 220 1254

Christ Church
Rathgar Road
Dublin 6
Tel: 01 496 6184

A local network of voluntary Christian Aid teachers is available to schools to help: take assemblies; use Christian Aid resources in class; support work on development issues, learning from religions and global understanding.

Contact your nearest office, listed above, for a Christian Aid Teacher to visit your school.

Development Education Association (DEA)
3rd Floor
29-31 Cowper Street
London EC2A 4AT

Tel: 020 7490 8108
Website: www.dea.org.uk

Provides information about local Development Education Centres.

Development Education Centre (South Yorkshire)
Woodthorpe School
Woodthorpe Road
Sheffield S13 8DD

Tel: 0114 265 6662

Fairtrade Foundation
Suite 204
16 Baldwin's Gardens
London EC 1N 7RJ

Tel: 020 7405 5942
Website: www.fairtrade.org.uk

Fairtrade Mark Ireland
Carmichael Centre
North Brunswick Street
Dublin 7

Tel: 01 4753 515
Website: www.fair-mark.org

Oxfam
274 Banbury Road
Oxford OX2 7DZ

Tel: 01865 311311
Website: www.oxfam.org.uk

Save the Children
17 Grove Lane
London SE5 8RD

Tel: 020 7703 5400
Website: www.savethechildren.org.uk

Traidcraft Exchange
Kingsway
Gateshead NE11 0NE

Tel: 0191 491 0591

UNICEF
55-56 Lincoln's Inn Fields
London WC2A 3NB

Tel: 020 7405 5592
Website: www.unicef.org.uk

1: Growing up

This unit introduces children to the concept of the growth and development of different aspects of an individual, for example physical change, emotional maturity, skills and responsibility. It explores the idea that these different aspects grow and develop at different rates within an individual and also between individuals; just as in any one person physical and emotional growth may not keep pace, so rates of development between individuals often vary.

Introductory activities

These introductory activities stress the importance of an individual's name and look at naming traditions from different cultures and countries. They contribute to an understanding of similarities and differences between individuals and encourage mutual respect. They also provide opportunities to discuss pet names, nicknames and name-calling.

Name-share game

The child has the right to a name and a nationality. The state must ensure the implementation of this right, in particular where the child would otherwise be stateless.

The UN Convention on the Rights of the Child (1989) Article 7

For each of us, much of our identity is closely linked to our name. Often the first thing a child learns to write is their name.

Preparing the class

A few days before the activity explain to the class that they are going to discover more about each other's names. Have a few copies of baby-name books so that children can look up the meanings of their own names (see Further resources page 9). Children could also ask parents, grandparents or other relatives if appropriate.

Learning outcomes	You will need
Children will: ★ learn about names, their origins and how names may change as we get older ★ learn to consider why getting names right is important.	A copy of the Name-share sheet and pencil per child. A few copies of baby-name books, preferably ones which include names from other cultures.

For example:

Jasmine (also *Yasmine, Yasmin*): from the plant name, also a late 19th-century name taken from Persian via Old French

George: Old French, taken from Latin and originally from Greek meaning 'farmer'

Thomas: from the Bible, originally Aramaic, meaning 'twin'

Whitney: from the surname, originally from the place-name meaning 'white island'.

If appropriate, ask children to find out, if they can, why their name was chosen (family tradition, religious belief, named after someone, parents' preference, etc).

NB: This may be a sensitive issue for some children and parents so you may want to alert parents before beginning

this activity. If children are adopted, parents may want prior notice of what they will be asked. If you feel this activity may be difficult and painful for children in care or for those neglected by their families, just have a classroom-based activity using baby-name reference books to look up name meanings and origins.

Sometimes people who settle in the UK change their name to help understanding or to avoid discrimination; HRH the Duke of Edinburgh's uncle changed his German name from Battenberg to Mountbatten because of anti-German feeling after the First World War. Many Irish and Jewish people changed their names after immigrating into the UK.

Name-share game – Name-share sheet

Call me	Note this about my name
Edward	Edward means successful protector. I used to be called Teddy when I was very small. I think I would like to be called Ed when I am a grown up.
Call me	Note this about my name
Call me	Note this about my name
Call me	Note this about my name
Call me	Note this about my name
Call me	Note this about my name
Call me	Note this about my name
Call me	Note this about my name

1: **Growing up** – introductory activities

How to play the Name-share game

1 Give each child a Name-share sheet and then go through the example on the sheet and discuss how it should be filled out. Check that everyone has something to say about their name before starting.

2 Ask each child to fill in the first box on their Name-share sheet for themselves. They should also include information about any changes to their names, ie 'baby' forms of their names.

3 Children then move around the classroom with their sheet and a pencil and exchange their information with each other until they have filled in all the boxes.

Discussion

Ask the following questions to start discussion.

● *If you found two or more people with the same name, did they have different things to say about it?*

● *Did anyone like the meaning of their name? Why?*

● *Did anyone not like the meaning of their name? Why?*

● *Has anyone's name been changed? Did they mind? For example, Amrutha to Achu; Peter to Pete; Christine to Chris.*

● *Did anyone's name change as they got older? For example, Petey to Peter; Rosie to Rosemary; Dichu to Vishal. Why did these names change?*

● *If anyone could make up their own meaning for their name, what would they choose?*

Continue to explore the difference between pet names, nicknames and name-calling. Talk about naming traditions and the right to a name. Explore why people might want to change their name and introduce the idea of changing name by deed poll.

Source: Centre for Global Education

 ## Taking names away

The Nazis tried to obliterate identity and sense of self by branding numbers on the arms of Jews in concentration camps during the Second World War. The book *The Number on My Grandfather's Arm* (see Further resources page 9) is useful in this context.

 ## Naming traditions in Ghana

In Ghana, West Africa, where one of the spoken languages is Twi, children are often named after the day of the week on which they were born. All the weekday names are derived from the names of gods and have a male and female form.

Children could give each of their family a Twi name according to the day on which they were born.

Source: Adapted from *The Whole Child*, 1990. SCF/UNICEF

Ghanaian Twi names		
Days of the week	Male	Female
Monday	Kwadwo	Adua
Tuesday	Kobna	Abena
Wednesday	Kwaku	Akua
Thursday	Yau	Yaa
Friday	Kofi	Efua
Saturday	Kwame	Ama
Sunday	Kwasi	Essi

The Growing-up game

This class activity explores the different aspects of growing up and the factors affecting the rates of growth and development of individuals.

The class works in groups and the aim of the activity is to chart the progress through school of an imaginary person. It involves interaction through bartering using noises rather than language. Bartering involves trading goods and services in exchange for other goods and services, rather than for money.

The children's learning therefore occurs largely as they move about the classroom, interacting with each other and later through discussion and reflection on the experience.

This activity ends with a writing exercise – writing an end-of-school report – to summarise their thoughts and ideas about the growth and development of their individual imaginary person.

The Growing-up game considers the growth of an imaginary person over five years and involves five rounds of bartering for coloured blocks. The number of coloured blocks collected during each round determines the amount of growth of the person at the end of that round.

Description of the game

● The class should be organised into groups of six and each group assigned a colour.

● The game consists of five rounds of bartering for coloured blocks. Each round lasts for three minutes.

● Each round represents a year in the life of an imaginary person at school. The coloured blocks collected during each round represent the growth of that person. This growth is recorded on the Person sheet by colouring in as many squares as blocks collected.

● Bartering is carried out using noises of musical instruments rather than language for communication. Each group's colour corresponds to a musical instrument.

NB: If the class does not divide equally into groups of six, some children can be appointed as observers. It is important that the whole class understands and recognises the value of this role – see Role of observers.

Learning outcomes

Children will:

★ *understand that we all grow up as individuals, unique in every way; physically, emotionally, socially and intellectually*

★ *recognise that these physical, emotional, social and intellectual characteristics grow and change at different rates **within** individuals*

★ *be aware that these characteristics develop at different rates **between** individuals*

★ *see that a range of influences affect the way we grow and change.*

You will need

Tables and chairs for groups of six.

1x Person sheet (enlarged to A3) per group.

1x Noises sheet (A4) per group.

1x Noises sheet enlarged to a Noises wallchart (A3) per class.

Observer's sheets (A4) if required.

1 set of six pencils, all one colour, per group (each group has a different colour).

1 set of ten mixed-colour multilink or unifix blocks per child (it is essential that a group's set of blocks omits the colour of that group, ie if a group is blue, their sets should not include blue blocks).

NB: Children can make up the sets of blocks to save time. Make sure each group knows which is their colour and to omit that colour from their sets of blocks. Remove any spare blocks to avoid the temptation to use those instead of bartering for blocks!

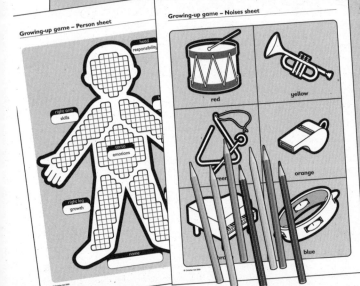

1: Growing up – core simulation

Role of observers

The observers' role is to observe the different interactions and ways of working within each group as they carry out the various tasks. It is a good idea to discuss this role with the whole class so that it is accepted as a vital part of the process. Time should be allocated at the end for the observers to report back on their findings.

Each observer should spend a round observing one group each, then move on to a different group for each subsequent round.

Preparing the class

Use the Person sheet to introduce the game.

Explain that the game is to help with understanding how people grow up as unique individuals.

Discuss the different types of growth and development of an individual according to the Person sheet, ie physical growth, skills, responsibility and emotional maturity. Ask children to think of situations that might affect each area of development.

For example, missing a lot of school because of an illness might mean that a person does not learn so many new skills during that year; moving house halfway through a school year may make a person feel frightened and left out for a while; breaking a leg in the summer term might mean not learning cricket or long-jump skills that year.

Use the following questions to help in the discussion on growth and development.

● *What can you do now that you could not do five years ago?*

● *What might you be able to do in five years' time that you cannot do now?*

● *Do you think you will stop growing and changing at some point in your life?*

● *What and who has helped you to grow up and will continue to do so?*

Discussing growth and development

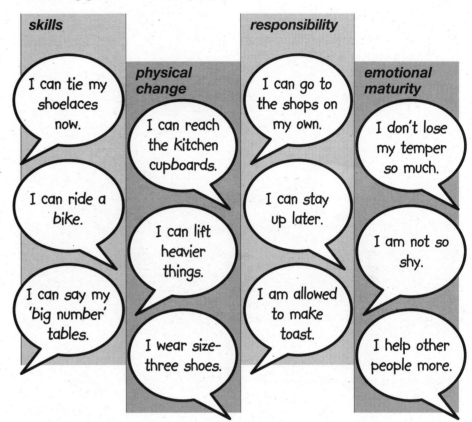

As these questions are discussed, think about the following as important factors for growing up and developing:

● family, friends, love and support
● food and exercise
● learning and doing
● opportunities and experiences.

NB: Some of these factors may be difficult and painful for some children. An alternative could be to relate these to school life, ie support and friendship for each other; school dinners and PE for food and exercise, opportunities and experiences that school life provides.

Suggest each group gives their imaginary person a name and each group member chooses a part of the body to colour in (for example head, left arm, right leg, etc) at the end of each round. Only the person responsible for the head may colour in the head at the end of each round.

Explain that to make their person 'grow' each child needs to collect coloured

blocks, and that the number of coloured blocks collected determines the number of squares coloured in at the end of each round. At this point, introduce the concept of barter, ie trading goods for goods, not money, and discuss how the interaction it requires and involves can symbolise the interactions an individual needs in order to grow and develop.

Explain that the children can only communicate during each bartering round by making the noise of their group's musical instrument – ie the red group makes the noise of a drum to let other children know they want to collect red blocks.

Use the Noises wallchart to make sure everyone knows which colour is linked to which instrument and let each group practise making their noise for others to guess. The aim of this method of communication is to have fun while, at the same time, appreciating the value of language for communication!

1: **Growing up** – core simulation

How to play the game

1 Give each group:
1 copy of the Person sheet
1 copy of the Noises sheet

Ask each group to colour in the instrument section on the Noises sheet that matches their coloured pencils. Make sure the Noises wallchart is up and visible to everybody.

The growth and development of individuals is dependent on a variety of factors such as: interaction with and support of family and friends; healthy diet and lifestyle; the chance to learn from others – such as teachers, peers, family; and the opportunities to experience situations, both positive and negative.

Just as we barter for things in everyday life, for example swapping a packet of crisps for an apple, so we can get and provide many of the aspects of growth and development through everyday contact and interaction with other people.

As different people have different experiences of these factors, so they grow and develop at different times and at different rates to become individual and unique.

Round one:
first year of school life

2 Explain that each child (except observers) moves around the classroom with their set of blocks, making the noise of their group's instrument. They collect blocks of their group's colour by swapping blocks with other children. They can only exchange one block for one block with any one player, then both must move on. If a player cannot collect their own colour, they can collect another colour and use that to swap with someone else.

NB: A demonstration of swapping and re-swapping colours beforehand will help explain the process.

3 After three minutes of bartering, the children return to their tables and each counts the number of their coloured blocks. They can then colour one square for each block collected in their colour and make the part of the person they are responsible for 'grow' as they colour in the squares. For example four red blocks equals four squares coloured in red.

Round two:
second year of school life

4 Switch round the pots of coloured pencils so that each group has a new colour. Make sure no group has the same colour twice in the activity. Ask the children to colour in the corresponding instrument on their Noises sheet and practise the sound.

5 Repeat the round as in 2 and 3.

● Remind the children that each round represents one year of school life. The coloured squares indicate a person's growth over the year. The new colour in each round enables children to see more clearly if there are differing rates of growth each year – ie each round.

● Review the growth of each group's imaginary person. Are different parts of the body growing at the same rate? Ask children to imagine events that might have happened to their imaginary person to explain their progress.

Discussion

Discuss the following questions with the class and then allow time for further discussion within the groups:

● *If your imaginary person has not got on well with others this year what might have caused this?*

● *If your imaginary person is more sensitive about their own and other people's feelings, what might have caused this?*

● *Has your imaginary person developed many skills this year? What might they be? How and where has your imaginary person learnt them?*

● *Has your imaginary person developed the qualities of responsibility – honesty, reliability and doing right – this year? What might have happened to encourage or hinder this?*

● *How much has your imaginary person grown physically this year? What might have happened to affect this growth?*

Encourage each group to share their ideas about their imaginary person with the class.

NB: children may talk about very personal experiences which will need to be handled sensitively.

Hindrances to growth and development

She was in hospital for six months because of a very bad accident. She will have to work much harder next year.

He didn't start to make any friends this year because he moved house twice in the year so he couldn't settle in.

Source: Ben, Luke, Andrew and Alex. Year 5, Hambleton C of E Primary School, North Yorkshire

1: Growing up – core simulation

Suggestions for co-operative report writing

Explain that each group is going to write a co-operative report on their imaginary person using the game of consequences as a model.

1 Give each child a blank sheet of A4 paper and a pencil and tell them to write their name at the bottom of the sheet.

2 Each child should write one or two sentences at the top of the paper to say how their imaginary person has done over five years in the area for which they are responsible, for instance skills, emotions, physical growth or responsibility. They should include reasons why and recommendations for help if appropriate.

3 They fold over the paper to hide the sentence(s) and pass it to the person on their left.

4 Each child then writes again about how their imaginary person has progressed in their area of responsibility. This does not have to be an exact copy of the first sentence.

5 Repeat the process until each child receives their own sheet back.

6 Unfold the sheets and, in turn, each group member reads aloud the sentences to the rest of the group. The group can then discuss the different versions and how they are going to produce a final report.

They may need to:

● change the order of some sentences

● change words

● remove the person's proper name where it occurs too frequently and replace with a pronoun

● add more sentences or link some together

● organise the sentences into paragraphs.

7 Each child can then amend their own copy and produce a final report. The group can produce a joint report by selecting elements from the individual reports.

Rounds three to five: subsequent years of school life

6 Repeat the process for the last three rounds and briefly assess the progress at the end of each. Remind the children that even after five rounds (years) their person is still growing, so not all the squares will be coloured in. Stress the ongoing process of growth and development.

Ask again what the children think they will be able to do in five years' time and to suggest what their imaginary person might be able to do in the future. What will they need to help them achieve this?

7 After the final round, ask each group to prepare an end-of-school report for their imaginary person. Each report should stress the imaginary person's strengths, recommend help for the weaker areas and explain why their imaginary person has done well, badly or maintained progress in the area for which they are responsible.

8 Ensure that any observers have an opportunity to tell the class what they noticed.

The co-operative report

She was really unhappy; her dog died and she couldn't concentrate at school

She really got on well at sports; her sister helped her to practise...

Growing-up game – Person sheet

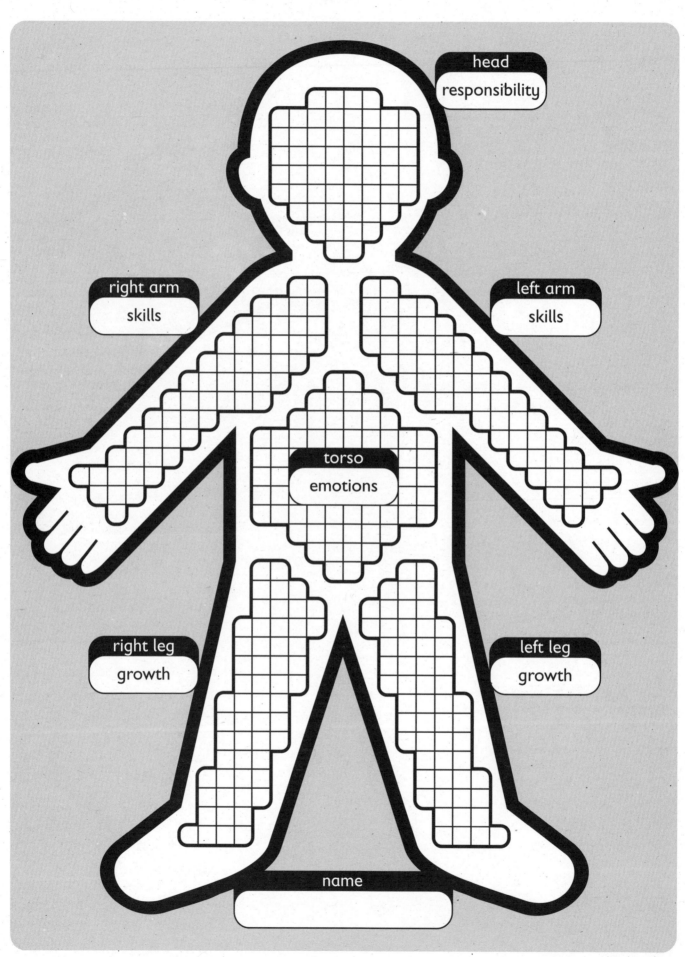

head
responsibility

right arm
skills

left arm
skills

torso
emotions

right leg
growth

left leg
growth

name

Christian Aid 2000

Growing-up game – Noises sheet

red

yellow

green

orange

brown

blue

Growing-up game – Observer's sheet

How did people choose which part of the body they wanted to colour in?

☐ people chose what they wanted

☐ one person decided for everybody

☐ the group decided by talking together

☐ other

What else did you notice?

....

....

How did people decide to start the colouring?

☐ one person started colouring, the rest waited

☐ one person decided for everybody

☐ the group decided by talking together

☐ other

What else did you notice?

....

....

Did people understand what they had to do?

☐ everyone understood quickly

☐ people helped each other understand

☐ some understood quickly, others did not

☐ other

What else did you notice?

....

....

How did people colour their squares?

☐ one at a time

☐ two at a time

☐ all together

What else did you notice?

....

....

How did people start bartering and collecting blocks?

☐ people wanted to start straight away

☐ some people were worried about what to do

What else did you notice?

....

....

How did people talk about their imaginary person's growth at the end of the round?

☐ people listened to each other

☐ one person had all the ideas

What else did you notice?

....

....

1: **Growing up** – follow-up activities

Growing up around the world

Preparing the class

Have a brainstorm session on what children are allowed to do now that they were not a few years ago. Discuss how they feel about these new responsibilities. Are there things they would like to do now but cannot? Are there differences between what girls can do and what boys can do, or between families?

Give each group an envelope containing the Claiming rights strips and ask them to read each statement. They then decide, as a group, at what age between birth and 18 years each activity is legally allowed.

The group then draws an Age-rights line – similar to a time line – and places each statement where they think it should go on the line.

When each group has finished they can explain their reasons for their Age-rights line to the whole class.

Ask the following questions.

● *Who decides what is the right age to do something?*

● *Do people stick to the age at which they can legally do things? If not, why not?*

● *Is it fair that you have to be a certain age to do things?*

● *Are children given enough or too much responsibility at each age?*

Compare the class Age-rights line to the legal ages in England and Wales – see right. If the class ages are different, discuss the reasons. Do they want to change any of the ages? What effect would that have? Is age the best way to decide when people can do certain things?

Source: Adapted from *Our World, Our Rights* (see page 9)

Learning outcomes	You will need
Children will: ★ *learn about the ages at which they can legally claim certain rights.*	One copy of the Claiming rights sheet for each group of five or six children, cut into strips. One envelope for each group into which is placed one set of Claiming rights strips.

Age-rights line

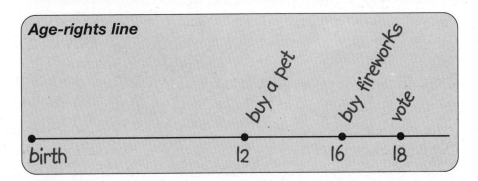

At this age

in England and Wales...

5	You must start school full-time.
10	You can be convicted of a crime if you knew it was wrong.
12	You can buy a pet without an adult with you.
13	You can get a part-time job (no more than two hours on a school day or Sunday).
14	You can go into a pub but not buy or drink alcohol.
16	You can buy fireworks without an adult with you. You can legally change your name. You can get married with your parents' agreement.
17	You can legally drive a car or motorbike.
18	You can vote. You are an adult by law. You can get married without your parents' agreement.

around the world...

Argentina
6	Start school.
18	Vote.
21	Marry without parents' agreement.

Kenya
5	Start school.
18	Marry without parents' agreement. Vote.

France
6	Start school.
18	Marry without parents' agreement. Vote.

Turkey
6	Start school.
18	Marry without parents' agreement (younger with parent's consent). Drive a car.
19	Vote.

Japan
6	Start school.
20	Marry without parents' agreement. Drink in a pub. Vote.

Growing up around the world – Claiming rights

✂ ···

When must you start school full-time?

···

When can you be convicted of a crime
if you know it's wrong?

···

When can you buy a pet on your own
without an adult with you?

···

When can you get a part-time job
(no more than two hours on a school day or Sunday)?

···

When can you go into a pub but not buy or drink alcohol?

···

When can you buy fireworks without an adult with you?

···

When can you legally change your name?

···

When can you legally drive a car or motorcycle?

···

When can you vote?

···

When are you an adult by law?

···

When can you get married with your parents' agreement?

···

When can you get married without your parents' agreement?

Growing up – Case studies

North India:
Madan's story

Madan lives with his family in Kharondi, a village in the north of India. His father's name is Paltan Ram. Paltan could not find enough work to afford to feed the family. One day, men came to the village offering to teach Madan how to weave carpets so he could earn money.

The men took Madan to Nadini, a far-away place, where he and other boys spent every day weaving in a shed. Madan's small fingers were good at knotting the wool around the threads on the weaving machine. The machine is called a loom. A good weaver could tie about 9,000 knots a day.

Madan and the others had to work 12 hours every day for seven days a week. There were no windows in the shed, just narrow slits and there was a plastic sheet in the roof for light. The factory was surrounded by high concrete walls with broken glass on the top to stop people getting out or in. The boys only had rice and thin lentil stew to eat, and they were punished if they stopped work by talking or laughing. The weaving cut the boys' fingers, twisted their backs and hurt their eyes. Fluff from the wool made their skin itch and got into their lungs. Life was very hard and Madan was never paid any of the wages he had been promised.

Back at home, Madan's father was looking for his son. He contacted an organisation called Mukti Pratishthan, which helps to save children from slavery in the carpet factories. The police also help because child labour is illegal in India. Mukti Pratishthan found out where Madan was working. So Paltan and some of the other boys' parents went with the police to make a surprise raid on the factory. The cruel factory owner tried to hide the children in an overgrown field nearby but the police found them. Madan, skinny and pale, came out of the long grass and fell into his father's arms.

Mukti Pratishthan helped all the children and their families to get over the horrible experience. Madan is now back at home, he goes to school and has time to laugh and play like other children. He wants to be a teacher.

Nicaragua:
Chela's coffee beans

Ten-year-old Chela Maria Padilla is an expert bean-sifter. She can spot a bad coffee bean before you can say 'milk, no sugar'. Sorting beans is her favourite job. Chela lives on a coffee farm, high in the hills of Nicaragua in Central America. During the coffee-picking season, Chela helps her mum and dad with the harvest. She gets up at 5am to help her mum sweep and make breakfast. It's often still cold and misty when she leaves to go to work. After filling her basket with beans from the coffee bushes, Chela sorts them into sacks.

Chela's family didn't earn much money from selling their beans. Sometimes they could not afford to pay for food or clothes, or to go to school. But now, with the help of a new coffee called Cafédirect, that's all changed. Cafédirect pays farmers a fair wage for their coffee beans so families like Chela's have enough money to buy things they need. Watch out for Cafédirect in the supermarket. It may have been made from some of Chela's beans.

Christian Aid 2000

Growing up – Case studies

Children speak out

From 28 May to 1 June 1998, more than 200 children from all over South Africa met together at Somerset West, Cape Town. They came from different communities and backgrounds, from villages, towns and cities.

They met to take part in the International Summit on the Rights of Children in South Africa. They wanted to speak for all the children of South Africa, including homeless and disabled children.

At the Summit, children talked about their problems and how they should be cared for and protected. They talked about the future and building a better life for all children in their country. The children talked, listened, shared, played and sang for four days. At the end they came up with The Children's Charter of South Africa.

As soon as they had written their Charter, these children began to take action. They spoke to other children and adults about the Charter. They presented it to political organisations, churches, community groups, trade unions, women's groups and the police. These children will not stay quiet about their rights. They are making their voices heard.

South Africa's children speak out

We came to the Summit to fight for the rights of children. Our rights are being ignored by the government and adults. Our demands are that we want all of the rights of children to be observed and applied by the government, adults and the communities.
Nkosi Banda

The Charter tells us about the rights of children and how we should be protected from abuse and violence. We want all the children of South Africa to know their rights.
Patricia Mbrabalala

The Summit was not all fun and games; we had many meetings where we discussed children's rights. This wasn't the least bit boring, in fact it was very interesting and I also learnt many new things.
Caleb Kenyon

Source: From International Summit on the Rights of Children in SA

2: Word house

This unit encourages children to think about the importance of language and its origins and development. It shows how our everyday language contains words and phrases from other cultures around the world.

Word-house game – Word-house sheet

Learning outcomes

Children will:

★ *learn that the English language is extended and enriched through contact with other languages*

★ *learn that there are many different languages in the world, with more than 300 spoken in the UK alone*

★ *learn that languages 'travel' as people move about and migrate.*

Introductory activities

Different types of messages

These three circle activities consider language and its use in communication.

Preparing the class

Choose and read a story that explores how mistakes happen through difficulties of communication (for example *The Surprise Party* and *Don't Forget the Bacon* by Pat Hutchins, see Further resources page 9). Use it to stimulate discussion of similar experiences. Then play the following circle games.

1 *Pass the squeeze*

Everyone holds hands in a circle. A message of squeezes (for example one long and three short) is passed round the circle. Did the same message come back to the 'starter'? Repeat with different patterns of squeezes.

2 *Alphabet messages*

Everyone sits in a circle facing right so that each person is facing someone's back. Choose one child to draw a letter of the alphabet with their finger on the back of the person in front. This tactile 'message' is passed around the circle until the last person draws it on a piece of paper, or the board for everyone to see. Has it changed? Why?

3 *Telephone*

Choose one child in the circle to whisper a brief message (for example 'I like pizza' or 'I went shopping yesterday') to the person on their right. The message is passed around the circle until the last person says it out loud. The aim is for the message to remain the same. A word from another language, preferably the first language of a class member, can also be used. This can help those who speak English as a first language to empathise with those who have the challenge of learning English as a new language.

● Discuss what would make it easier to pass on messages. This is also a good opportunity to discuss communication through: sign language, Braille, Morse code, the telephone, the Internet and e-mail. How do people manage to communicate when they do not speak the same language? How did sailors pass messages from one ship to another before they had radio? How do they communicate now? How might they in the future?

25

2: **Word house** – introductory activities

 *Only one language*

This story considers why there are so many different languages and dialects in the world.

Tell the Choctaw story to the class and use the following questions to stimulate discussion.

Discussion

● *Have you heard this, or a similar story, before? (For example, the Babel story from the Bible, which is about 3,000 years old.)*

● *Why do you think the Hebrew people and the Choctaw people tell these stories?*

● *Why do you think people do not all speak the same language?*

● *What word describes someone who speaks: one language? (monolingual); two languages? (bilingual); more than two languages? (multilingual).*

● *How many languages can you say hello, goodbye and welcome in?*

● *Do you know any songs in another language?*

● *What could you do if you were able to speak more than one language?*

Follow-up

Write the Choctaw story as a poem or present it as a short play or a presentation for an assembly. Or illustrate it as a poster or story book.

The Choctaw Story

This is a story told by the Choctaw Indians, who live in North America. The story explains why people around the world speak different languages.

Many, many years ago, Aba, the good spirit in the sky, created many men and women from the yellow clay of the earth. All the people were Choctaw and spoke the Choctaw language. They could understand each other.

One day they all came together and looked up at the sky. They wondered what the clouds and the blue above might be. They kept talking among themselves and at last they decided to try to reach the sky. So they started to build a big tower of rocks to reach the heavens.

But one night there was a very strong wind. The wind was so strong it blew the pile of rocks over. The next morning, when everyone started to talk to each other, they were amazed. They could not understand each other. Some people could still speak the language of the Choctaw and these people became the Choctaw tribe. The other people, who could not understand this language anymore, began to fight each other. In the end they split up and went to different parts of the world.

Source: Adapted from Farb, Wordplay quoted in *The Languages Book,* 1981

2: Word house – core simulation

Word-house game

Modern English, which is more than 500 years old, is the result of progressive additions and influences from other cultures and languages. Starting with the arrival of the Angles, Saxons and Jutes to Britain in the fifth century, it is a record of past links with the wider world – both of people migrating in, bringing with them their languages, and of British people emigrating and living in other countries.

This development of language is a continual and dynamic process as new discoveries are made and new influences experienced.

This whole-class activity, based on the concept of 'language families', enables children to explore the diversity of linguistic influences. Children work in pairs, each representing a family from another country and all living in the same street to symbolise the variety of language influences on English. The activity is in two parts and so may take place over different lessons.

Preparing the class

Ask the class to imagine it is made up of families from eight different regions of the world that have influenced the English language. The classroom is 'Our Street'. The families live next door to each other in a row of terraced houses. The eight different families are Celtic, Dutch, French, Greek, Indian, Italian, Roman and Scandinavian. Split the class into pairs and give each pair a Family word card.

NB: There will be more than one pair in each family but family pairs should not sit together.

The Word-house game looks at the influence of different cultures on the development of the English language. The class, working in pairs, researches the meanings and use of words that have influenced English. Pairs interact with other pairs to share words and build their own word bank.

Learning outcomes	You will need
Children will:	Tables and chairs arranged so that children can work in pairs, and are able to move around the room.
★ **understand that the English language has adopted words from other languages, giving it a rich international flavour**	One Family word card per pair.
	One A4 Word-house sheet per pair.
★ **know something about the origins of words**	Enough coloured pencils for each family to have a different colour (pairs within the same family have the same colour).
★ **be able to offer a reason why particular words have come into the English language**	A large number of strips of paper (approx 4cm wide) for writing sentences on.
★ **have practised dictionary skills**	
★ **be able to demonstrate that they understand the meaning of selected words.**	One A4 sheet of white paper per pair to make a family sign.
	One dictionary per pair.
	Children's reference books for research on cultural backgrounds of the different families.

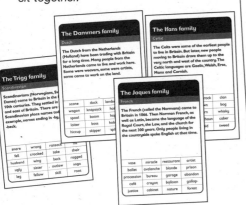

2: **Word house** – core simulation

How to play the Word-house game

Part one

1 Each Family word card has 20 of the many words their language has contributed to the English language. Ask the children to use the reference books to find out something about the cultural background of their family and to record it along with their family name and country of origin on the A4 sheet of paper. They could design a family sign or logo to decorate the sheet.

2 Give each pair a copy of the Word-house sheet. Using their family colour, the children colour the bricks containing the words from their Family word card. They also write their family name and cultural group on the front door.

3 Ask the children to research and write down the meanings of their family words using a dictionary so that they know what each word means and how it can be used. They will need this knowledge later in the game.

Here is a natural break if one is needed.

Part two

Explain that people learn the languages of other groups and facts about their countries through contact with people. The aim of this part is for each pair to 'visit' and meet the other family groups in order to get as many bricks coloured in as possible.

4 Give each family a handful of the paper strips. Ask each pair to choose a word they have not coloured in and, on the strip of paper, write a sentence to show what it means. For example 'I need an **umbrella** when it rains'. They can use a dictionary to help if necessary.

5 One person from each pair then takes their sentence containing their chosen word and their family Word-house sheet around the other families to find out which country or cultural group the word comes from. When the right family is found, the visiting person shows that family their sentence. If the family thinks the word is correctly used, they colour the corresponding word brick on the visitor's Word-house sheet using their own family colour. The visitor takes it home.

6 Meanwhile, the other member of the pair stays at home with their Family word card to check visiting families' words and their correct use. They then use their family colour to colour the appropriate bricks on the visiting family's Word-house sheet.

7 When the visiting member of the family returns, the pair make up another sentence and swap roles so that each person gets to visit. They continue taking turns until all the bricks are coloured in, or time is up.

Discussion

Discuss the activity and what the children have learnt. Discuss the multicultural nature of the English language and the resulting variety of words. Also the dynamic nature of language and the influences of travel and time.

This activity only uses eight of the language groups which have influenced English, but newer sources also contribute words. Ask children to list words from other sources that are now part of the English language, for example e-mail, Internet, website, microchip, laptop, online, download, CD-ROM, fax, software, modem, multimedia, megabyte.

Alternatively, remove one word from each of the Family word cards and from the Word-house sheet. Replace these words on the Word-house sheet only with eight 'new' words from the above list. At the end of the game, these will not be coloured in and so can lead to discussion on how technological developments can also contribute to the development of a language. Emphasise that these words are not from one cultural group but are as a result of new technology.

Further ideas

The Word-house sheets could be displayed together as a row of terraced houses. The class can then illustrate the street's surroundings to give it an international feel. The display can be a basis for creative and imaginative writing.

NB: While the selection of words from each cultural group has been made in good faith, they may not all stand up to detailed etymological study. This is not important in the context of the game which is primarily to do with appreciating the rich international flavour of the English language.

Word-house game – Word-house sheet

buffoon	macintosh	balloon	veranda	shamrock	uproar	bungalow	coracle
take	chutney	medium	crooked	garage	January	studio	blonde	café
periscope	ransack	crayon	cushy	gymnasium	pedestal	lavatory	pendulum

atom	spool		leg	boss			ugly	crag
fungus		leprechaun			hobble
luck	glen		dekko	loot			cairn	boom
procession		forest			gallop
bairn	bible		druid	cycle			pucka	album
landscape		nature			jockey
beck	piano		devil	dock			loch	root

chapatti	crisis	wrong	prison	genius	sister	victory	angel
caber	animal	hiccup	gymkhana	groove	agenda	bureau	anonymous	bog
miracle	shampoo	concert	skipper	ragged	curry	opera	balcony
dirk	stiletto	carnival	acrobat	cheetah	macaroni	bangle ·	abandon	pizza
restaurant	orchestra	galore	crown	splint	circus	wagon	snare
wing	ballet	alphabet	volcano	character	recipe	inferno	cabinet	miser

giant		justice				sponge
exit	clan		thug	myth			yoga	down
dungarees		spaghetti			outlaw
hit	vase		saga	hoist	
confetti		catamaran	
scone	kirk		skill	rich	
attitude		umbrella	
their	place		hope	pyjamas	whisky	educate	corridor
avalanche		fellow	museum	chorus	church
deck		fell	telephone	jungle	dinghy	school
	tweed	husband	loiter	traffic
	solo	knapsack	theatre	artist	street

Christian Aid 2000

Word-house game – Family word cards

The Trigg family

Scandinavian

Scandinavians (Norwegians, Swedes and Danes) came to Britain in the 8th, 9th and 10th centuries. They settled in the north and east of Britain. There are still many Scandinavian place names today. For example, names ending in -by, -fell and -beck.

snare	wrong	ransack	hit
fell	crooked	take	their
husband	wing	beck	ragged
ugly	sister	outlaw	saga
leg	fellow	skill	root

The Dammers family

Dutch

The Dutch from the Netherlands (Holland) have been trading with Britain for a long time. Many people from the Netherlands came to live and work here. Some were weavers, some were artists, some came to work on the land.

scone	dock	landscape	deck
wagon	knapsack	hoist	rich
spool	boom	hope	groove
loiter	boss	hobble	luck
hiccup	skipper	splint	uproar

The Ifans family

Celtic

The Celts were some of the earliest people to live in Britain. But later, new people moving to Britain drove them up to the very north and west of the country. The Celtic languages are Gaelic, Welsh, Erse, Manx and Cornish.

crag	cairn	shamrock	clan
loch	coracle	down	bog
macintosh	glen	bairn	whisky
galore	dirk	leprechaun	caber
kirk	jockey	druid	tweed

The Jaques family

French

The French (called the Normans) came to Britain in 1066. Then Norman French, as well as Latin, became the language of the Royal Court, the Law, and the church for the next 300 years. Only people living in the countryside spoke English at that time.

vase	miracle	restaurant	artist
ballet	avalanche	blonde	prison
procession	bureau	garage	abandon
café	crayon	balloon	gallop
justice	cabinet	nature	forest

Word-house game – Family word cards

The Theodore family
Greek

During the 5th century BC, Greece was ahead of most of the world in topics like science, art and philosophy. Many Greek people were artists, scientists and philosophers (thinkers). When the Romans invaded Greece many soldiers started to use parts of the Greek language. The Romans brought many Greek words with them when they invaded Britain in AD43.

crisis	museum	angel	gymnasium
acrobat	telephone	atom	theatre
character	devil	bible	orchestra
myth	alphabet	periscope	anonymous
cycle	church	place	chorus

The Benedictus family
Latin

The Romans invaded Britain in AD43 and stayed until AD418. Their language, Latin, was used by schools and colleges for over 1,000 years. It is still used and taught in some schools and universities today.

crown	recipe	January	exit
fungus	educate	giant	animal
pendulum	album	street	lavatory
circus	school	sponge	miser
genius	agenda	medium	victory

The Giovanni family
Italian

The Italian language became popular during the 16th century because of the art and music of Italy. Many rich Britons visited Italy to enjoy the architecture, paintings and music and brought back some of the Italian language.

opera	concert	spaghetti	piano
confetti	umbrella	studio	stiletto
carnival	solo	volcano	pedestal
traffic	inferno	macaroni	pizza
balcony	attitude	buffoon	corridor

The Kallie family
Indian

Many Indian words from languages like Hindi, Gujarati, Bengali, Punjabi and Tamil became part of the English language during the 19th century when Britain ruled the continent of India. While the Britons were living there, they adopted parts of the language and brought them back to Britain.

curry	chutney	dungarees	loot
bangle	bungalow	thug	dinghy
veranda	yoga	cheetah	pyjamas
cushy	jungle	shampoo	pucka
chapatti	gymkhana	dekko	catamaran

2: Word house – follow-up activities

Leaving home: other countries

This activity encourages children to think about the migration of people, a concept children will encounter when studying places and processes as part of the geography curriculum. The influence of language is not always included in these but can add a valuable extra dimension. The activity involves children moving around the class collecting information from each other.

Preparing the class

Explain that the children are to move around the class, asking each other the questions on the question sheet. They record the answers on the sheet and then move on to the next person. They cannot ask the same person more than one question.

Discussion

Use the following questions and ideas to discuss the results of this activity.

● *How many different countries are recorded? Are any the same as those in the Word house activity?*

● *How many are European countries?*

● *How many are from other regions of the world?*

● *Has anyone in the class ever visited another country? Which language was spoken? Did everyone speak the same language?*

● *Why do people move from one country to another?*

● *What things might you notice when you arrive in a new country?*

● *How could your community help strangers feel welcome?*

Source: *Migration*, M Davies and *Mangla – a study of change and development in Mirpur, 'Azad' Jammu Kashmir and Pakistan*, Development Education Centre (South Yorkshire)

These follow-up activities explore the influence of one language on another that occurs as people move about the world.

Learning outcomes	You will need
Children will:	**One Leaving-home questionnaire per child.**
★ *consider the reasons why people migrate*	
★ *think about what it is like to arrive as a stranger in a new country.*	

Why do people move from one country to another?

The following are suggestions.

● **To find work**

● **Freedom from ill-treatment such as abuse and torture**

● **To get a higher education**

● **To escape a natural disaster – eg volcanic eruption**

● **To take control over more land and wealth**

● **A way of life – eg nomads and travellers**

● **Because lands and homes have been taken over – eg by a reservoir or dam project**

● **To escape war or famine**

● **To look for a new life**

● **To earn more money**

● **To recruit more people to follow a religion**

● **To stay with or live near relatives and friends**

● **To improve opportunities for children**

● **To help people in need**

● **To live in a better climate**

Leaving home – Leaving-home questionnaire

Write the name of a person in your class who:

1 has lived in another country . . . .
The name of the country is . . . .

2 has a parent from another country . . . .
The name of the country is . . . .

3 has a grandparent from another country . . . .
The name of the country is . . . .

4 has visited another country . . . .
The name of the country is . . . .

5 has had visitors from another country . . . .
The name of the country is . . . .

6 writes to somebody in another country . . . .
The name of the country is . . . .

7 has received a postcard from another country . . . .
The name of the country is . . . .

8 knows someone who travels and
works in another country . . . .
The name of the country is . . . .

9 can say something in a language other than English . . . .
For example, say hello, count or sing a rhyme
The name of the language is . . . .

Christian Aid 2000

2: Word house – follow-up activities

 ## Leaving home: refugees

Refugees are people who have fled from their own country in fear of being persecuted because of their religion, nationality, membership of a social group or for a particular political opinion. Some people may leave to escape war in their country. In 1995 there were 18,094,000 refugees throughout the world – many of them were children.

Throughout history there have been refugees, for example as a result of the Highland clearances in Scotland in the early 1800s, and the potato famine in Ireland in the 1840s.

Refugees who arrive in the UK and Ireland do not necessarily speak much English. They are met at the airport or seaport by immigration workers who help them fill in the forms which they need in order to live in this country until the government agrees they can stay. If they do not speak the language, this can be very difficult. Refugees wanting to settle in new countries are called asylum seekers.

This activity aims to give children an insight into the language experiences and difficulties that refugees and asylum seekers often face when they first arrive in a new country.

Preparing the class

Organise the class into groups of four and ask them to imagine they have fled their home in fear, and are running for their lives. They arrive in a new country that they hope is safe, but they do not speak the language and are confused. They have been asked to fill in a form which is written in Turkish. Discuss what questions the form might ask, then ask each group to try to fill it in.

Discussion

Use the following questions to discuss the activity.

● How did you feel?

● Were you confident you got the form right?

● Were you confused, fearful?

Then ask the groups to compare their result with the English translation.

How accurate were they? Explain that if they get any details wrong or change any details later, their story might not be believed. If they passed through another country they could be returned at once to that country to seek asylum there.

Remind the class that the questionnaire was written using a Roman alphabet, like English. How much more difficult would it have been if it had been written in a different script?

Leaving home – Asylum-seeker's questionnaire

1 Isim

Soyadi

2 Cinsiyet ☐ Erkek ☐ Kadin   **3** Dogum Tarihi ☐ / / ☐

4 Adres

Şehir

Ülke

5 Pasaport numarasi

6 Beraberde getirilen çocuklarinizin sayisi?

Isimleri	Cinsiyetleri	Yaşlari

7 Ingiltere'ye nasil geldiniz?

☐ Uçakla   ☐ Gemiyle   ☐ Eurostar'la

8 Ingiltereye direk olarak mi geldiniz?
Eğer başka ulkede durakladiysaniz, hangi ülkede.

9 Ingiltere'ye geimenizin nedeni?

10 Kendi ülkenizi terketmenizin nedeni?

11 Dokümanlar
Talebinizi destekleyen hangi dokümanlariniz var?

Talebinizi destekleyecek olan başka kanitlariniz var mi?

Source: Adapted from an idea by Amnesty International-UK

Leaving home – Asylum-seeker's questionnaire

1 First name

Surname

2 Gender ☐ Male ☐ Female

3 Date of birth [/ /]

4 Address

Town

City

5 Passport details

6 Have you any accompanying children?

Names	Genders	Ages

7 How did you come to the UK?

☐ Plane ☐ Boat ☐ Eurostar

8 Did you come directly to the UK?
If you stopped on the way, where did you stop and when?

9 Why are you coming to the UK?

10 Why did you leave your country?

11 Documents
What documentary evidence have you got?

What other evidence have you brought with you?

Source: Adapted from an idea by Amnesty International-UK

Word house – Case studies

Eritrea:
Selam's story

Selam is a refugee from Eritrea.

Important people

'I love my mum and dad and I miss them – especially my mum. Even though she may be dead she will always be important to me.

My friend Rahwa is 15 years old. She is in Asmara, in Eritrea. She is important to me because we were like sisters. We used to talk about everything and understand each other. We also used to go out and have fun. I really miss her.

My friend Aida (here in London) is 23 years old. She reminds me of my friend Rahwa. I can talk to Aida about everything; I feel comfortable with her.

I think friends at school are important because some of them are refugees like me and sometimes when I feel depressed they are able to understand and share my feelings. I feel better when I talk to them.

Life in Britain

Friends here help me to speak English and learn new words. But I don't want to forget my own language – Tigrinya. Speaking my own language means I won't forget where I come from.

I love my foster family in England – they are wonderful. I wanted only love and support but I got much more than I expected. My foster brothers and sisters take me to different places that I can enjoy like youth clubs, funfairs and the seaside. I don't like being alone here because I get bored and start thinking about my own family. Then I feel sick that I haven't got any family left.

I like the freedom I have here. If I want to go out on Saturdays I can, but in Eritrea I couldn't even go to my friend's house.

I don't like English food because I only ate hot spicy food back home and if I eat English food, I feel as though I haven't eaten anything. I don't like the weather because it is too cold in winter. It doesn't rain much in Eritrea but here it rains even in summer.

School in Eritrea and England

I went to an Italian school in Asmara, the capital city of Eritrea. I learned Italian and Tigrinya, as well as maths, science and geography. I stayed there until 1995. I really enjoyed going to an Italian school because I've always liked to learn different languages.

When I came to England I was really amazed by the way the students behaved. Back home, students were very well behaved. Once we got to our class, we didn't talk until the end of the lesson unless we had to ask the teacher a question.

In my country, schools are quite good except that many have been destroyed by the war. At my school, classes were big, about 40 students, but in England they are quite small, about 20 students. The one thing I like about English schools is that we have dinners. In Eritrea, students have to go home for dinner.

My future

I am leaving school next month. I am hoping to pass my GCSE exams and go to college to study leisure and tourism. I am looking forward to carrying on with my studies, getting a degree and having a job one day.

My other dream is to go back home to visit Eritrea and find out if it is safe to stay there. If things have changed, I would like to play a part in the development of my country. I would like my country to become a peaceful place. Sometimes I say that if things haven't changed, I will have to stay in England. I think I will feel sad that I can't go back, but part of me will always be in Eritrea because I belong to that country.'

Christian Aid 2000

Word house – Case studies

Mamo's Story

'I live in Sierra Leone in west Africa. My country has had a war for many years. My family and I had to leave our village, Bunumbu, because we were afraid we might be killed when the rebel soldiers attacked.

I am a ten-year-old boy and I live with my mother, father and two sisters – Massah who is five and Amie who is only nine months old. My grandmother and aunts and cousins also live with us. We live in a camp now, but not everyone in our family is registered, so we don't all get food rations. We have to share what we have among us all. There is not enough to go round.

Because we had to leave our village in a hurry and then walk a long way, we could not bring much with us. Our bucket to collect water is too small. That is a problem. We have been given blankets, a cooking pot and a lamp – these help but it is difficult not having enough to eat and drink. At home we ate rice with vegetables. Here in the camp we have bulgur wheat. It looks a bit like rice, but tastes different. I like rice better and so do my friends.

There is a school in the camp that I will go to when term starts, but I'd rather go home. My father says we can go when the government tells us it is safe, but it will be hard to find somewhere to live or food to eat. Our house and fields will have been destroyed.

I have friends here in the camp. I play hide-and-seek and football with them and sometimes we dance too. My little sister likes dancing.'

Christian Aid 2000

3: Global cake

This unit introduces children to the concept of world trade, looking in particular at producers and consumers, fairness and fair trade. Although children often find these ideas difficult, they affect children's lives on a daily basis through the food they eat or the clothes they wear.

Introductory activities

These three short activities explore children's ideas of fairness and unfairness.

That's not fair!

● Ask the children to raise their hands if they have said 'that's not fair' in the last week.

● Working in groups of two or three, ask the children to think of two incidents if possible – one in school and one out of school – where they felt something unfair happened – and to share them in their groups.

● Share some of the incidents with the class including what seemed to be the cause of the unfairness.

● List the things the children find unfair and their ideas about how to deal with the incidents more fairly.

Mountain-bike race

Make sure the class understands the use of gears on bikes and that:

● a high gear is useful on flat ground as it allows you to go fast while you pedal slowly

● a low gear allows you to pedal fast up a steep slope to keep going without falling off.

Divide the class into pairs and give them the following information.

Marilyn and Kofi can both ride a bicycle well and both are fit and healthy. They have hired bikes and are going to race each other, but each bike only has one gear.

RACE 1: one kilometre and very flat all the way	*RACE 2:* one kilometre straight up a steep hill
Marilyn's bike has one very *high* gear. Kofi's bike has one very *low* gear. Both start off at the same speed. *Who is most likely to win the race? Who is going to use more energy? Is this a fair race?* Give reasons for your answers.	Marilyn suggests she and Kofi swap bikes. Marilyn's bike has one very *low* gear. Kofi's bike has one very *high* gear. *Who is going to find it harder to pedal uphill? Who is most likely to win the race? Who is going to use more energy? Is this a fair race?* Give reasons for your answers.

3: **Global cake** – introductory activities

Fist or palm

How to play the game

Divide the class into pairs; each child chooses to be 'A' or 'B'.

Explain the following rules without using the words 'winning' or 'losing' and do not in any way imply that this is a competition, although some may think it is.

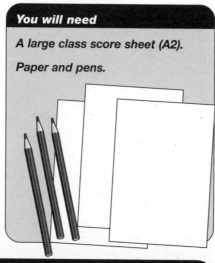

You will need

A large class score sheet (A2).

Paper and pens.

Round 1:

This round is played in complete silence. Only the teacher may speak.

1 Partners face each other with their hands hidden, either under the table or behind their backs.

2 When the teacher signals, players show their partner either a clenched fist or an open palm.

3 Each pair keeps its own scores according to the score sheet.

4 Repeat this ten times and ask for scores. Has anyone scored over 30? Anyone under 20? Do not comment.

Round 2:

This round can involve discussion and children can decide together what moves to make and take their ten goes in their own time. Children record their scores. Ask for scores and discuss the following questions.

● *Did they think they were competing and wanting to win; or were they helping each other to solve a problem? Why?*

● *Did pairs operate differently during the second round?*

● *If there was no discussion on the moves, why not?*

● *Did anyone agree a move and then do differently?*

● *Did any pair try to get scores that were more equal?*

● *What was it about the game that could lead to unfair or very unequal scores?*

Score sheet

A	**B**
1 (fist)	**1** (fist)
2 (palm)	**2** (palm)
4 (fist)	**0** (palm)

Source: Christian Aid, *It's Not Fair*, 1993

3: Global cake – core simulation

Global-cake game

The aim of this whole-class activity is to produce a wall mural of a global cake, where the children are cooks baking a communal cake.

The class, divided into nine groups, represents the world's population and the cake's ingredients represent the world's resources. The nine different-sized groups represent nine regions of the world and are divided proportionally according to the population size of each region. Each region is responsible for providing an ingredient for the global cake, for example eggs, butter, flour, etc. But each group has only one type of equipment (for example glue, scissors, etc) with which to produce their ingredient. So they have to trade and interact with other groups to get what they need. Through this negotiation, children explore the fact that different countries of the world are connected by trade and that this does not always benefit people equally.

Through the Global-cake game children explore international trade as they bake an imaginary global cake. The class is divided into different sized groups, with each producing a poster of an ingredient for the cake. Each group must barter to get the resources needed to produce their poster.

Learning outcomes

Children will:

★ **learn that countries of the world are linked together through trade**

★ **learn that international trade does not necessarily benefit consumer and producer equally**

★ **learn that hard work is not always rewarded with fair and just pay**

★ **learn that some people have to work very hard just to survive**

★ **learn something of the location of the world's population**

★ **learn how charity and justice affect people.**

An important learning element involves the children moving around the classroom, negotiating for items they need to complete a task.

You will need

Nine groups of tables and chairs (see page 42 for arrangement).

An instruction sheet per group.

An ingredient symbol sheet per group.

Resources for the task (page 42).

A1 sheet of paper per group (flipchart size).

Four arrow templates on card.

A large world map on the wall for reference (atlases or a globe are also useful).

Labels with the name and colour of each group's region.

A real fruit cake* (bought or made in advance – see page 42 for recipe) and cut into the same number of slices as children taking part. Hide from view until needed.

*a large bar of chocolate or packet of biscuits can replace the cake.

3: Global cake – core simulation

Table A: Resources

Region	Resource	Colour
Asia (excluding East Asia)	9 x A4 thin card	yellow
Africa	9 x glue sticks	purple
South and Central America (including the Caribbean)	9 x world maps	light green
Western Europe	2/3 pencils in each of the colours in the list	brown
North America	9 x scissors	red
East Asia	4 x arrow templates	orange
Russia and Central Asia	9 x lead pencils	black
Eastern Europe	9 x blue pencils	pink
Oceania	A5 paper for ingredients and group label	dark green

Table B: Number of chairs and slices of cake for a group of 35

Region	Chairs	Slices of cake		Proportions
Asia (excluding East Asia)	10	0.5	For groups of sizes other than 35 divide the number of pupils in the group by roughly the proportions given at right or use your own judgment.	35%
Africa	6	0.5		20%
South and Central America (including the Caribbean)	4	2.5		15%
Western Europe	4	9		15%
North America	3	9		10%
East Asia	2	5		5%
Russia and Central Asia	2	1		5%
Eastern Europe	2	2.5		5%
Oceania	2	5		5%

Cake recipe

Ingredients

170g butter or margarine
140g sugar
3 eggs
225g flour
1 teaspoon baking powder
3 dessert spoons milk
225g raisins
112g glacé cherries
3 nuts for decoration

Method

Cream together fat and sugar. Beat eggs and add to mixture. Sieve flour and gradually fold into mixture. Add baking powder with last spoonful of flour. Add raisins and cherries. Add a little milk but keep mixture fairly stiff to prevent fruit falling. Turn into greased 12cm tin and bake in a moderate oven for about 1 hour 20 minutes. Leave cake to cool for 5 minutes, then turn it out onto wire tray. Decorate with nuts.

3: Global cake – core simulation

How to play the game, including class preparation

● Allow the children to sit in friendship groups within the arrangement of chairs; however, they cannot move any of the chairs.

● Explain that this activity is to look at the way different countries of the world are connected by trade. To do this, the children imagine they are all cooks baking one 'communal' cake. The 'communal cake' will be in the form of a global-cake mural.

● The children represent the world population and are divided into nine different regions of the world.

● Each group is responsible for producing one of the cake's ingredients.

● Each group will produce an A1 poster of their ingredient to add to the global-cake mural.

● Groups must trade with each other for the equipment needed to make their poster.

● Allow each group, one at a time, to find their region on the large world map or globe (see page 64).

1 Discuss with the class what they would need to bake a fruit cake together – such as ingredients and equipment. It would be useful to have examples of these things in the class. Use the following as discussion points.

● How the amounts of each ingredient differ, some ingredients are needed in large quantities, but small quantities of other ingredients are equally vital to the success of the cake.

● How the balance of these ingredients is important.

● How the ingredients change on mixing and cooking to make something new that is good and useful to eat.

2 Explain that the imaginary cake is going to represent a 'global cake' where the world's resources are the ingredients and the world's people are the cooks.

3 Remind the class they are sitting in groups that represent regions of the world and each region is responsible for providing one ingredient for the cake – sugar, butter, eggs, baking powder, flour, milk, cherries, raisins, and nuts. Each group's ingredient is determined by population size, ie flour – the largest quantity of ingredient – is provided by Asia, the region with the largest population.

4 Each region has to produce an A1 poster with:

● their region's name

● a map with their region coloured in

● the right quantity of their ingredient, coloured and stuck on

● four arrows – to represent the processes of trading and production.

Have an 'already prepared' example to show the children.

5 Tell the groups that each region only has one type of equipment, for example scissors, to make their ingredient for the cake. This means they will have to trade any spare equipment with other regions to get the rest of the equipment they need. If any group runs out of spare equipment to trade they can use their barter units. Each group will have 16 barter units and each resource item has a price, for example a sheet of card costs 4 units.

6 Hand out instruction sheets to each child and go through each point to make sure everyone understands the game. Remind the children that the activity is about trading resources but if they run out of these, they can use their barter units. The teacher will take on the role of the UN in the event of disputes.

7 Allow time for the groups to plan their strategies – for example which resources they will need to trade for. Allow 30 minutes for trading and poster-making and give a ten-minute warning before the end of the game. Everyone must stop regardless of whether or not they've completed their poster.

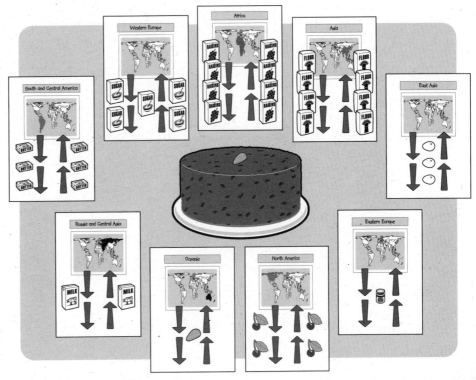

3: Global cake – core simulation

Discussing the mural

Put all the posters on the wall around the Fruit-cake sheet (see page 43) even if some are incomplete. Use the following to help with discussions.

● *What does the mural look like – is it complete?*

● *Why are some ingredients better prepared and mounted than others?*

● *Did the size of the group make a difference?*

● *How did each group organise to do the task?*

● *What was it like... in the large groups? ... in the small groups?*

● *How did they feel that some groups seemed to have an easier time than others – did it seem fair?*

● *How could the activity be made fairer?*

● *Did anyone have any free time – what did they do with it?*

Sharing the cake?

Remind the children that the cake represents the world's wealth (its resources and industry) and the groups represent the world's population. The group sizes were different because population size varies across the regions of the world. Some parts of the world are wealthier than others; they have more resources and industry. Explain that a real cake is going to be shared between the regions to represent how, in reality, the world's wealth is shared amongst its population.

Now bring out the cake and distribute it as described in Table B, page 42, making sure that no cake is eaten until the children have discussed how they feel.

Sharing responses

It is likely that there will be a spread of feeling; anger, frustration, dismay or disappointment among those who worked hard and received little; glee, relief and guilt among those who received lots of cake.

Encourage the children to share their feelings. Consider the question of fairness and ask for suggestions for solving the problem. Groups with a lot of cake could share with those who had little. Ask the children to consider how they feel about the amount of cake they get being decided by those willing to share. Rich countries often give help to poor countries. What happens if the rich countries have a bad year? Is this a fair arrangement? Does a one-off amount solve all problems? What about long-term help? Can children think of other ways in which the world's wealth might be shared out more fairly?

NB: Although it may not be the best solution for the world for the pieces of cake to be shared out by 'charity' rather than 'justice', it may be better for classroom relations to end the activity this way.

Rounding off

Tensions may have developed during this activity. It is therefore important to finish with a quick co-operative activity to bring the group together as a whole.

Four up

The object of this game is to have exactly four people standing at all times. Everyone starts by sitting down. Anyone can stand up whenever they want to but for no longer than five seconds at a time before sitting down again. Anyone can get straight up again if they want to.

Attribute linking

An attribute is called out and children quickly move around the room to join those with the same attributes. For example, call out 'birthday month'. Everyone calls out their birthday month and moves to join those with the same month. When everyone has joined a group, each group calls out their month one at a time. A new attribute is given and groups break up and move to form new groups. Suggestions for attributes: place of birth; countries or continents visited; favourite hobby, sports team, pop star, etc.

Variations: This could be repeated non-verbally with mime or sounds.

Source: Various

Global-cake game – How to make the Global cake

Region	Colour	What ingredient to make	Resources	Sell for (units)
Asia (excluding East Asia)	yellow	8 packets of flour	9 x A4 card	4
Africa	purple	8 packets of raisins	9 x glue sticks	2
South and Central America (including the Caribbean)	light green	6 packets of butter	9 x world maps	2
Western Europe	brown	5 packets of sugar	2/3 pencils in each of the 9 colours	6
North America	red	4 cherries	9 x scissors	6
East Asia	orange	3 eggs	4 x arrow templates	5
Russia and Central Asia	black	2 cartons of milk	9 x lead pencils	3
Eastern Europe	pink	1 tin of baking powder	9 x blue pencils	3
Oceania	dark green	1 nut	A5 paper to make ingredients and group label	5

Part 1

1 Imagine your class is the whole world. The class is divided into different groups and each group comes from a different part or region of the world. Your class is going to make an imaginary cake and each group has to make a poster with an ingredient for the global cake.

2 Use the table to find out what your region's colour is, which ingredient you are making and which resource you have. For example if your region is *Asia* your ingredient is *flour*, your colour is *yellow*, your resource is *card*.

3 You will need to:
● make a poster with eight packets of flour coloured yellow
● make four arrows from card to stick on your poster
● write your region's name on the poster.

4 To make your poster you will need to trade or swap your spare resources to get the other resources you need. For example, if your group is Asia you will have nine pieces of card so you can trade the eight pieces you do not need for the other resources you do need. Each resource is worth one resource, for example one pair of scissors is worth one pencil.
   If you run out of resources to trade with you can use your barter units to buy resources you need.

5 Collect everything you need to make your group's ingredient poster.

Part 2

1 Colour in your region on the world map with your coloured pencil, for example Asia is yellow. Use the big world map in your classroom to help find your group's region.

2 Make four arrows using the arrow template and card. Colour the arrows blue.

3 Get enough paper to make the right number of your ingredient.

4 To make your ingredient:
● first cut out the large picture of your ingredient, for example, packet of flour – this will be your template
● use the lead pencil to trace around it on sheets of paper and cut them out
● copy what is on the template onto your outlines of the ingredient and colour in with your region's colour.

5 When you have finished your ingredient, make a name label for your region. When you've finished making these, stick your ingredients, the name label and the arrows onto your poster. Now your part of the global cake is finished.

Do not forget, you must get all the things you need by trading with other groups.

Christian Aid 2000

Problems ahead

3: Global cake – follow-up activities

Through the core activity, children will have discovered that the world does not operate a fair trading system and that this contributes hugely to world poverty. To gain a better understanding of what life is like for people in poor countries, it is important to explore how people really live in a community. This links well with learning about different places in the world in the geography curriculum (see page 9 for useful packs to explore community life in other countries).

Problems ahead

This activity can help children understand how unexpected problems that some people can deal with and overcome may mean disaster for other people.

Learning outcomes	You will need
Children will: ★ **consider and start to understand how families who are just 'keeping their heads above water' are affected by unexpected problems.**	**A copy of page 46 so that each pair of children has either A or B.**

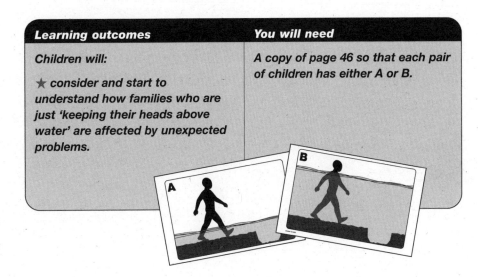

Preparing the class

Divide the class into pairs. Give half of the pairs picture A, and the rest picture B. Ask each pair to discuss what they think will happen to the person in the drawing (page 46) when they reach the hole. How far up the person will the water reach? How can they show this?

The children then form groups of four so that both A and B parts of the drawing can be seen together.

Discussion

Discuss with the class what they think the saying 'keeping our heads above water' means. Why do people use it when life is difficult? Explain that for many people who are poor or homeless – like refugees – life is like walking through deep water; it is hard to keep going and even a small problem can become a big crisis.

Ask the children to think of problems that might affect people in this country, for example:

● losing a job

● unexpected illness in a close family member who lives far away

● equipment breaking down, for example, fridge, TV, heating or car.

What problems might affect people in poorer countries? For example:

● storm damage (hurricanes, floods, landslides, etc)

● drought in farming communities

● paying to see a doctor

● paying to go to school.

Are there ways in which richer countries help their own citizens in difficulty? For example unemployment benefit, housing benefit, child benefit, National Health Service, etc. Why do these not exist in poorer countries?

Key to pictures A and B

Water = difficulties in daily life

Hole = unexpected problem

3: Global cake – follow-up activities

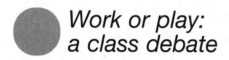

Work or play: a class debate

Preparing the class

Explain that there will be a statement shown to the whole class. Each child should read it carefully without discussing it with anyone. They should decide whether they agree or disagree with the statement or do not know. They should also think of reasons for their decision.

How to play the game

1 Once children have decided what they think about the statement, they select a badge to show their view, either *agree, do not know,* or *disagree.*

2 Each child then moves around the class to find someone who is wearing the same badge and they discuss why they both chose that badge. What are their reasons? What kind of work were they thinking of?

3 After a few minutes, they look for someone who is wearing a different badge and find out why they chose their badge. At any time, if the other person's reasons make them change their mind, they can change their badge using a pen.

4 After a few minute's discussion, they move on to find someone wearing the third kind of badge and share their reasons. Once again, they can change their label if necessary.

5 At the end, everyone returns to the original person they spoke with and shares the different reasons they have heard.

6 The class can now sit in a circle and discuss the different perspectives and ideas on the statement.

This can be written up as two sides of a debate or used as preliminary preparation for a class debate.

Source: Centre for Global Education. Adapted from Pike and Selby, *Tackling a Statement in Human Rights – An Activity File,* 1988 (now out of print)

Learning outcomes	You will need
Children will: ★ **learn to articulate their own point of view** ★ **learn to listen to different perspectives** ★ **learn to prepare for a class debate.**	Sticky-label badges; make equal numbers of each badge, totalling a few more than the number of children in the class (see below). A poster or OHP acetate with one of the following statements. 'No one should be allowed to do paid work while they are a child.' or 'Children should not be expected to pay towards the family budget.' or 'Most children will learn more from going out to work than from going to school.'

Child Labour: key facts

● Up to 250 million children worldwide work for a living – one out of every four children in the developing world.

● Of the 190 million working children aged 10 to 14, three-quarters work a six-day week and half work more than a nine-hour day.

● There are growing numbers of children at work in the United States and in Europe – 5.5 million aged between 12 and 17 in the United States alone.

● The South Asian Coalition on Child Servitude estimates that there are 55 million child labourers in India – the equivalent of the entire population of the UK.

Source: *Christian Aid News,* winter 1997

Global-cake – Case studies

Columbia:
Manuel's story

'I am nine years old. My name is Manuel and I live in Bogotá. Bogotá is the capital of Columbia. My brother, Luis, and I work in the greenhouses of a big company that grows flowers to send to other countries. Some go to the UK and Ireland. The flowers that grow in the greenhouses are carnations, roses and lilies. We send flowers to the Netherlands too. Sometimes they get Dutch labels put on them. My job is to water the flowers. I use a big heavy hose. It is hard to do. Luis sometimes has to tie knots in nylon twine to keep the plants upright. My boss likes children to tie the knots because they have small fingers and can do the job quickly; but the nylon cuts into our skin. The boss does not pay us as much as the grown-ups. It's so he can make more money. We often get sick because they spray the flowers with pesticides. The spray makes us dizzy and sick. It's against the law for children to work with pesticides because they are dangerous chemicals, but not all bosses obey the law. We don't even have masks or gloves to wear so lots of us – the grown-ups too – are ill. We can't go to school and our families need the money. Even with the money we earn, we can't always eat. Who would believe that the lovely flowers in the shops and markets in your country would cause us children so much suffering.'

Adapted from 'Withering of the Flower Children'. *The Observer* 9 July 1995

England:
Craig's story

'My name is Craig and I live in Sheffield. I am 11 years old and besides going to school, I earn money by doing five different jobs. On four days I get up at 6.30am to do a paper round. I get up at 5.30am on Thursdays and Fridays because I help with a milk round. That is, until I fell off the milk float and broke my leg. That was a bit of a blow as it was in plaster for four weeks and I couldn't do any jobs at all. Usually on Saturday mornings I help in a neighbour's clothing shop from 10am to 12noon, then I help out at the second-hand furniture shop next door with furniture removals. On Sunday I work in the local take-away restaurant from 12noon to 2pm. So I work for about ten hours every week and usually earn about £5. I enjoy having some money to spend but I do feel tired, especially at school. It's nice to stay in bed a bit longer at the weekend.'

Source: *The Hidden Army,* Pond and Searle 1991

Global-cake – Case studies

Thailand:
Sawai's story

'My name is Sawai Langlah. I used to live in northeast Thailand but I had to move to Bangkok to find work when my father became paralysed. My cousin helped me to find a job in a factory that makes clothes.

There were 20 machines in the factory and 20 of us working there. If you looked at it from outside, you couldn't tell it was a factory. The windows were high up and had bars. We weren't allowed to open the windows. No one could see in from outside. The other workers were between 15 and 17. We worked six days a week. The factory was supposed to follow government rules. The owners were very unkind and mean. They didn't pay us much money. They didn't care.

Then I heard about the Child Labour Club that meets at weekends. I started going to classes there on Sundays. They also help children with problems and give health care and shelter. Now I work for the club part-time and I've quit my factory job. The club pays me a better wage than the factory and they gave me a room to share for no rent.'

Source: Adapted from Swift, *New Internationalist*. July 1997.

India:
Pintu's story

'My name is Pintu. I am 12 years old and I live in Uttar Pradesh in India. I work for a company that produces sports goods. These are exported to other countries. I help to tan the leather and do some stitching. In India you are not supposed to work until you are 14 but my family needed the money to be able to have enough food and clothes.

It is dangerous in the tannery where I work. There are sharp knives to cut the hide, the animal skins are heavy to lift and sometimes we get splattered with lime solution which is bad for the skin. Children aren't supposed to work in tanning at all – it's against the law, but some of us do.

I left school when I was ten to help my father in the tannery. He works from 7am to 7pm. I worked with him for six hours. I didn't get paid, but at least my father did not have to work longer hours. He earns £1.37 a day.

I stopped working in the tannery in April 1997 because the government held a survey of children working in dangerous industries. But I still need to work for my family.'

Source: Adapted from *A Sporting Chance*, Cottingham 1997

Christian Aid 2000

Global-cake game – Example poster for Asia

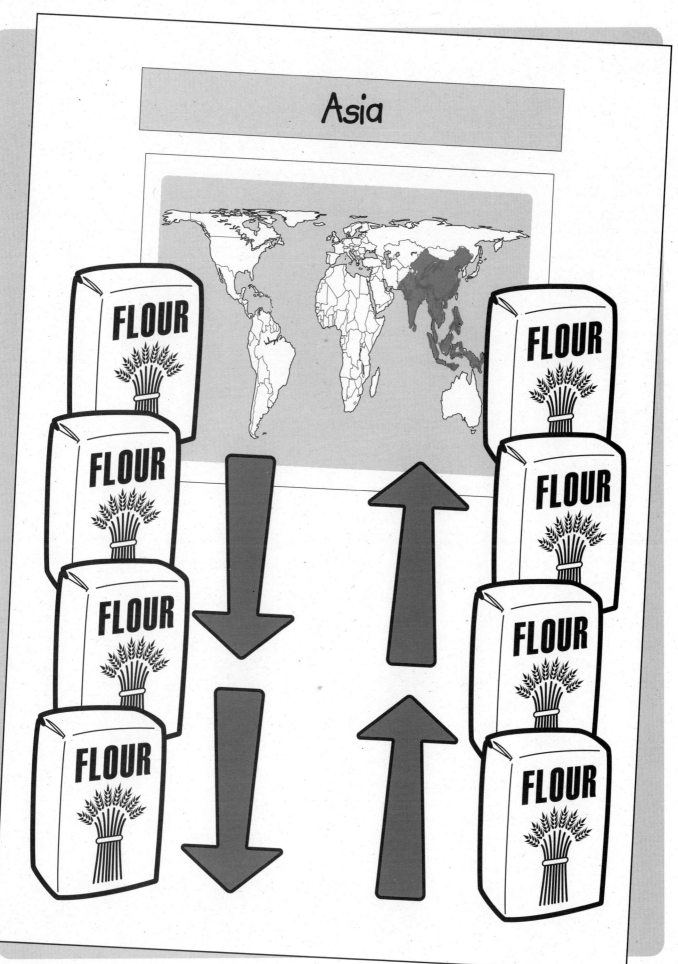

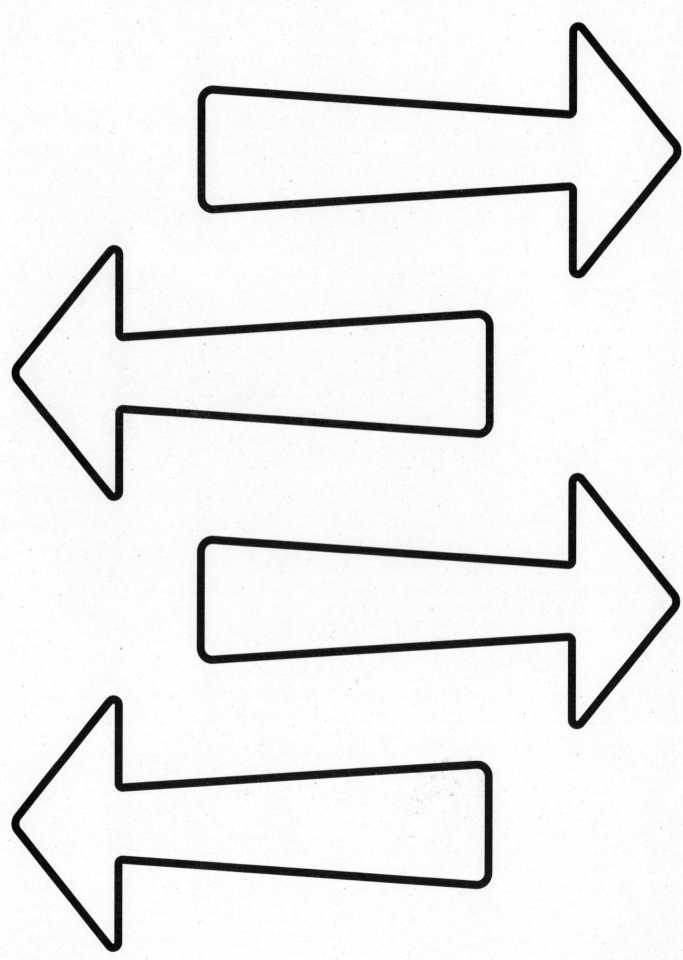

Global-cake game – World map

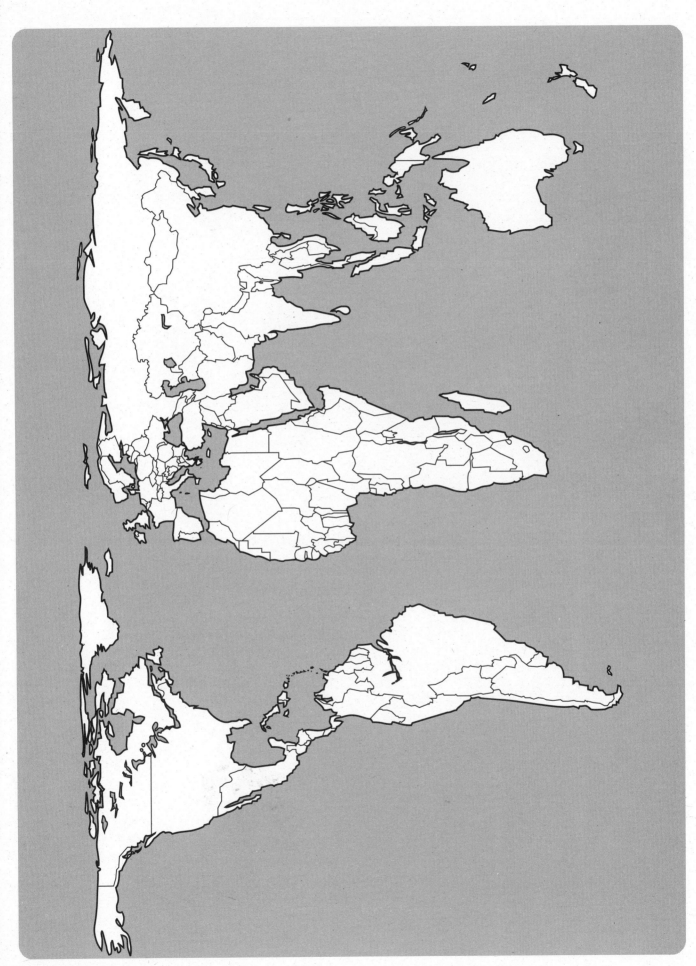

Global-cake game – Fruit-cake sheet

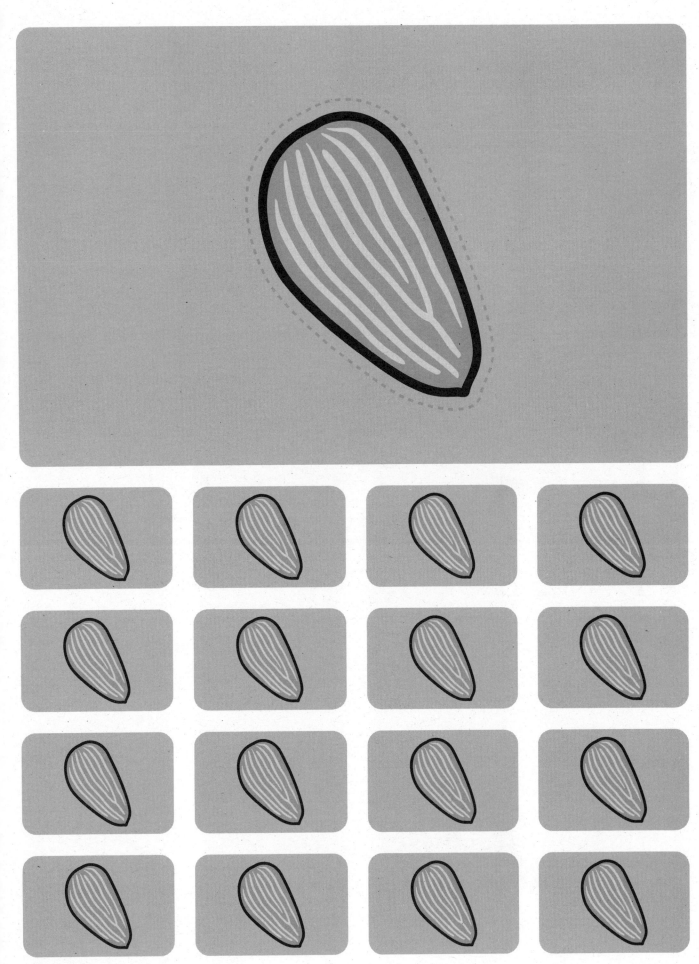

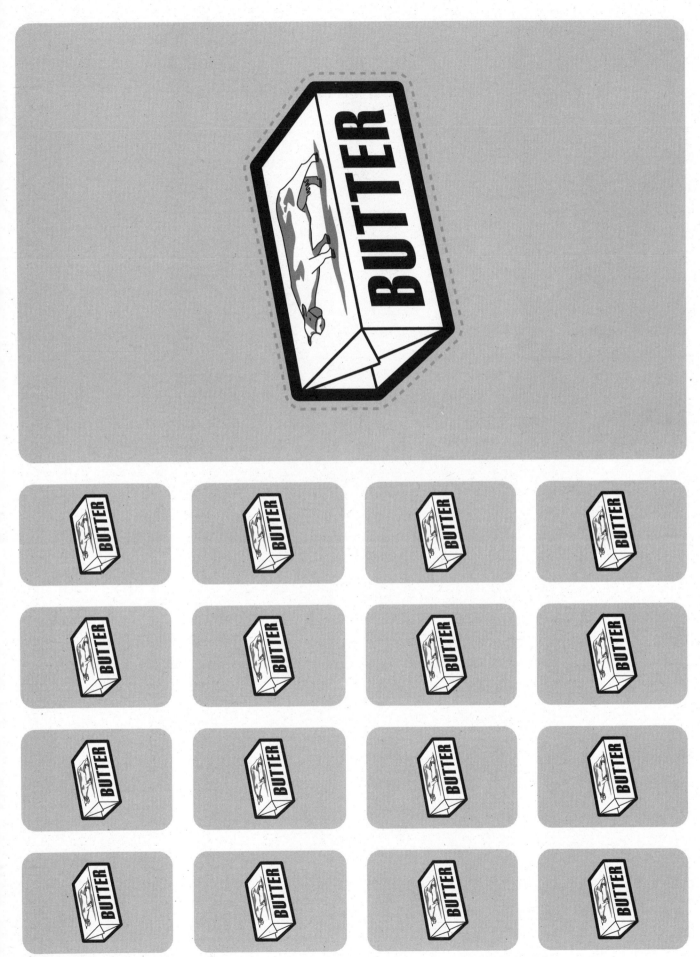

Global-cake game – Symbol sheet: Russia and Central Asia

Global-cake game – Symbol sheet: East Asia

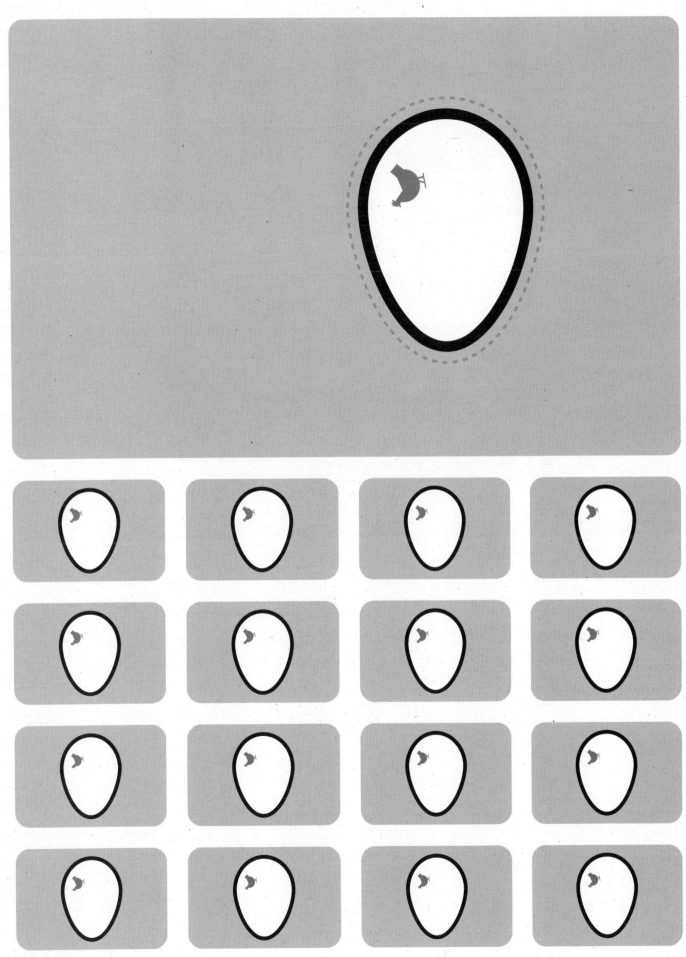

Global-cake game – Symbol sheet: Asia

Global-cake game – Symbol sheet: Africa

Global-cake game – Symbol sheet: North America

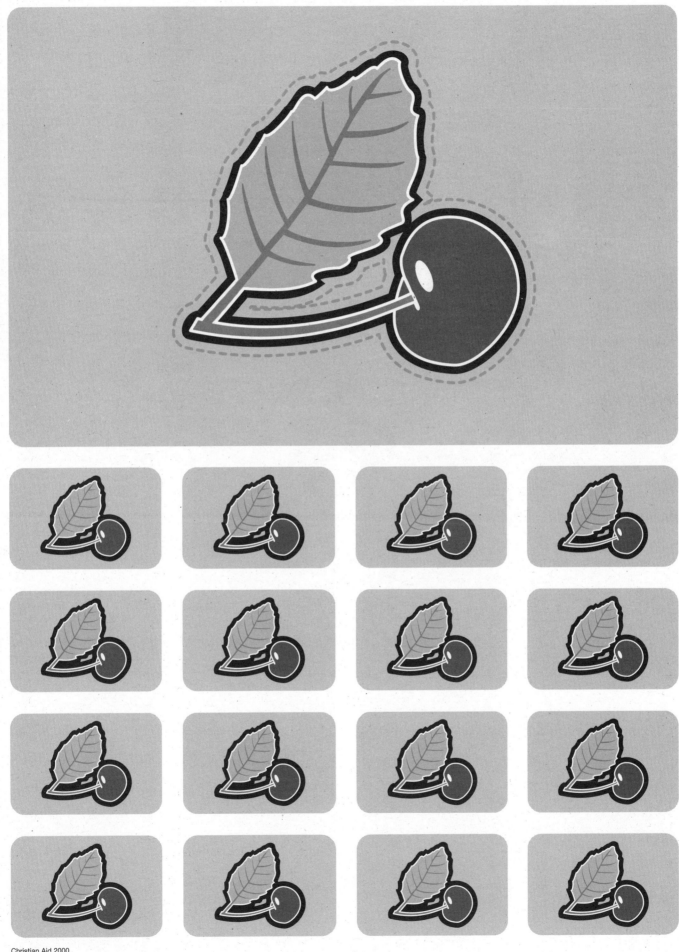

Global-cake game – Countries within each region

Asia (excluding East Asia)

Bangladesh
Bhutan
Brunei
China
Cambodia
India
Indonesia
Iran
Iraq
Laos
Macao
Malaysia
Maldives
Mongolia
Myanmar (Burma)
Pakistan
Papua New Guinea
Philippines
Singapore
Sri Lanka
Thailand
Vietnam

Africa

Algeria
Angola
Benin
Botswana
Burkina Faso
Burundi
Cameroon
Cape Verde
Central African Republic
Chad
Congo
Côte d'Ivoire
Djibouti
Egypt
Equatorial Guinea
Eritrea
Ethiopia
Gabon
Gambia
Ghana
Guinea
Guinea Bissau
Kenya
Lesotho
Liberia
Libya
Madagascar
Mauritania
Morocco
Mozambique
Namibia
Niger
Nigeria
Rwanda
Senegal
Sahara
Somalia
Sudan
South Africa
Swaziland
Tanzania
Tunisia
Togo
Zambia
Zimbabwe
Zaire

South and Central America (including Caribbean)

Anguilla
Antigua and Barbuda
Aruba
Barbados
Bahamas
Bermuda
British Virgin Islands
Cayman Islands
Cuba
Dominica
Dominican Republic
Guadeloupe
Haiti
Jamaica
Martinique
Montserrat
Netherlands Antilles
Puerto Rico
St Kitts and Nevis
St Lucia
Trinidad and Tobago
Virgin Islands

Western Europe

Austria
Belgium
Denmark
Finland
France
Germany
Iceland
Ireland
Italy
Luxembourg
Netherlands
Norway
Spain
Sweden
Switzerland
United Kingdom
Turkey
Greece

North America

Canada
United States
Greenland*

East Asia

Hong Kong
Japan
North Korea
South Korea
Taiwan

Russia and Central Asia

Afghanistan
Azerbaijan
Kazakstan
Kyrgyzstan
Tadzhikistan
Turkmenistan
Uzbekistan
Armenia
Russia

Eastern Europe

Bulgaria
Estonia
Hungary
Latvia
Lithuania
Poland
Romania
Slovakia
Slovenia
Croatia
Czech Republic
Ukraine
Belarus
Bosnia-Herzogovina
Former Republic of Yugoslavia
Macedonia
Albania

Oceania

Australia
New Zealand
The islands of Polynesia, Melanesia and Micronesia (including Fiji, Samoa, Tahiti, Tonga, Vanuatu)

NB: This list has been drawn up for the Global-cake game. It is not a definitive list of regions and countries.

*Although Greenland is part of the Realm of Denmark, it has been grouped according to its geographical location.

Christian Aid 2000